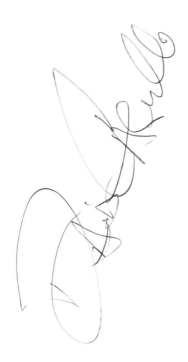

Leading
the
High-Energy
Culture

Leading
the
High-Energy
Culture

WHAT THE BEST CEOs
DO TO CREATE AN
ATMOSPHERE WHERE
EMPLOYEES FLOURISH

DAVID CASULLO

PRESIDENT, BATES COMMUNICATIONS

New York   Chicago   San Francisco   Lisbon   London   Madrid   Mexico City
Milan   New Delhi   San Juan   Seoul   Singapore   Sydney   Toronto

1 2 3 4 5 6 7 8 9 10 DOC/DOC 1 0 7 6 5 4 3 2

ISBN   978-0-07-178126-8
MHID   0-07-178126-9

e-ISBN   978-0-07-178127-5
e-MHID 0-07-178127-7

McGraw-Hill books are available at special quantity discounts to use as premiums and sales promotions or for use in corporate training programs. To contact a representative, please e-mail us at bulksales@mcgraw-hill.com.

This book is printed on acid-free paper.

*To my grandfather, the most energizing leader
ever to impact me. And to my father, the most
genuine person I have ever known. Both live on
in my heart and soul.*

Contents

Acknowledgments

Energy that resonates is created by One, but is enhanced by many.

To list the multitude of family, friends, colleagues, teachers, coaches, and other extraordinary people who have blessed my life and amplified the energy inside me would be impossible. I am grateful to each and every one of you.

For the support, courage, and clarity to create this work, I feel so deeply grateful to:

My wife, Lori, and our three children Andrew, Jenna, and Sara—you are simply the most important people on earth.

Phil Martin—for his professionalism, his intellectual curiosity and debate, his example as a leader, and his friendship, all of which got me through this process. You're a fine man!

Scott Weighart—for his incredible ability to take concepts and help others think about them deeply and understand them clearly and for his genius for creating material that promotes true learning.

My brother—for his leadership of the family during this difficult period. You have always been my hero.

Neil Goldberg—for his inspirational leadership and phenomenal business sense and for giving me the opportunity to formally learn how to help build great leaders.

All my closest friends from business, for all their love and encouragement. It's easy to write about energizing leaders when you have them as dear friends and witness them in action daily.

John Sauer—the one man whom I know who lives the credo, "The true measure of a man is how he treats someone who can do him absolutely no good." I'm passing it forward, John.

Ken Lizotte—for giving it to me straight when I decided to become a published author, and for helping me achieve the goal.

My mother and father—for their ultimate example of "lives well lived."

And, finally, to Suzanne and Drew—for their willingness to share their wisdom, experience, and their home, and for their encouragement throughout this process. I am so blessed to have both of you as mentors and partners.

Leading
the
High-Energy
Culture

Introduction

> *In your hands . . . is the future of your world and the*
> *fulfillment of the best qualities of your own spirit.*
> —ROBERT F. KENNEDY, FORMER U.S.
> SENATOR AND ATTORNEY GENERAL

In my 27-year career in business, and even before this, growing up in a small town, I've always been drawn to leaders who energize me—truly great leaders who share a seemingly intrinsic quality that envelops their being with pure *energy* in such a way that people around them find themselves energized as well:

Neil G., CEO of a billion-dollar retailer, who assumed the reins when it was a small family-held business and grew it through his passion, commitment, and amazing business mind.

Kathy I., CEO of a multibillion-dollar empire dedicated to working mothers. She completely transformed her personal brand, which was enormously successful, because she believed in something deeper and more important. She energizes the very people who might otherwise resent her because her personal truths are so authentic and compelling that working mothers cannot ignore the power of her passion.

Greg H., managing director for the premier wealth management company in the world, who builds successful talent within the organization by taking a genuine interest in each person's development. He recalls how his father was always involved with his circle of friends when he was growing up, caring for their well-being, offering encouragement, sharing wisdom at the perfect time. This impacted his friends, but it impacted him more. He carries this torch now with his team and with his family in spite of the enormous demands of his profession.

Ed F., a vice president of sales, who took a languishing sales force in a lackluster distribution business and breathed life into it every day with his enthusiasm and desire to win. His ability to coach and inspire salespeople stemmed from something innate in his being.

Suzanne B., an entrepreneur, who built her business from nothing to a multimillion-dollar enterprise and learned along the way how to create, sell, and deliver a world-class portfolio of professional services. Her toughness is outdone only by her love for learning and genuine concern for those she attracts to her team with her vibrant energy.

Paul M., a high school social studies teacher and head football coach. His personal belief that "great accomplishments are not reserved for others" is a lesson he learned from his dad. He challenges himself as a leader to look for the gift in each of his students and athletes, whether they are exceptional or not. Then he helps to instill confidence so they will each have the courage to pursue their own blessing.

Kevin C., the chief technology officer for a rapidly growing municipal township in Colorado. Kevin's personal values so resonate with the unique mission of the town government he leads that he is able to consistently attract and retain top IT talent to his team. The extraordinary growth of the town stems, in part, from his leadership within this remarkable small government. Through Kevin's impassioned leadership, this small city government has become nationally recognized as one of the top U.S. Digital Cities in its category and as the recipient of a Best on the Web award.

Iris N., the director of executive education at a New England college. Mentored by an inspirational leader, Iris found within herself the courage and conviction to help women business leaders develop the skills and confidence to lead at the highest levels in their organization. Iris's energy amplifies the energy of all those involved in her organization's renowned Executive Education program, allowing them to compete with much larger, better-funded universities.

Michael O., the chief administrator for a small-market hospital that was on the verge of extinction. Michael believes that patient care begins and ends at the point of contact with the nurses, doctors, and staff who face the public. He leads from the front lines where these talented people work. His personal truths were formed at an early age on the farm where he grew up, and honed in the grocery business where minuscule margins are the reality. The fine line between success and failure, he learned, is determined by the quality of service that the people under his leadership commit themselves to deliver.

These leaders are real. They are special. And, unfortunately, they are rare.

This book is for you whether you are a highly accomplished leader, perhaps the CEO of a large company, or an emerging leader who wants to understand how the best leaders infuse valuable energy into their organization. This book will tap the power of their resonating energy inside you—an asset that when leveraged will propel you personally to new heights of leadership success. As important, when your amplified energy flows through your organization, your business and your people flourish. This book is a step-by-step process that explains how to drive your amplified energy into your culture to make your organization a "high-energy culture."

The intensive, experimental five-year leadership development program I was involved with demonstrated that this phenomenon is possible with *any* leader so inclined to develop himself. I know this because through our own Leadership Development Institute we saw people who were committed to their own development transform themselves into great leaders. This means you can, too.

Energy emanates from one extraordinary leader and resonates through other leaders, permeating the entire organization.

In every organization—a business, a department within a business, an athletic team, a volunteer organization, a government, a school, a hospital, or a family—resonance begins with the leader and must be sustained by the leader. Although the energy is innate, the leader creates resonance through the clarity of his personal truths, the atmosphere in his organization, and his powerful, timely, and effective *communication.* Only when the leader's behavior and words are aligned with his core personal truths does energy begin to resonate and have a stimulating effect. To prolong the effect, resonance must be intentional and pervasive and be deeply embedded throughout the organization.

Embedded resonant energy becomes powerful, and the organization in which it is present reaches the pinnacle of its potential and becomes a *high-energy culture.* When resonant energy permeates the culture of an organization, starting with the leader and flowing through other key members—internal and external—it creates a synergizing effect. This effect brings out the potential of all the individuals it impacts within the organization—customers, employees, vendors, investors. The leader of the high-energy culture is able to marshal the collective intellect and capability of all stakeholders and align them with his impassioned vision. In this culture, people are self-motivated to do their very best. Commitment in the high-energy culture is extraordinarily high. The people in this atmosphere of high energy flourish. The continued development of each individual in the high-energy culture has a higher return on investment than in organizations where this phenomenon is not at work, giving the high-energy organization an enormous competitive advantage. The synergy that results thus becomes the driving force for sustained, consistent high performance.

There is enormous economic value to this high energy!

There are other significant benefits too. In business, the energized culture creates marketing gravity and draws customers to the company. There is an attractive force to this energy. It attracts the best talent, because these people want to play on *your winning team*. Investors and bankers are more inclined to capitalize these businesses. They feel the energy and sense something special is going on. Vendors recognize this as well and act to ensure that they are the chosen supplier to your unique culture.

School systems that possess this energized culture enjoy teachers and administrators who extend themselves beyond the call of duty to assist students beyond the school day, contribute selflessly to curriculum review and development, voluntarily attend professional development activities, and constantly seek to improve instruction. They don't work by the clock but by the *calling* that is their profession.

Leaders who understand the power of their own energy and who act to leverage it are special and noteworthy, but this is "not reserved only for others." You have within you similar power to create a high-energy culture of your own. Your leadership potential is unlimited.

This book is for you, a leader in a position to lead an organization who wants to understand how this energy inside, that *already exists*, is tapped, amplified, and made to become enormously powerful to you as an impassioned and potentially extraordinary leader.

WHAT THIS BOOK WILL SHOW YOU ABOUT HIGH-ENERGY CULTURES

I am a practitioner. All the concepts are drawn from observations and actual experience over my long life and career. The power of the energy that resonates from leaders with the qualities I describe in detail is most vivid when I reflect on my life. Some examples I have experienced first-hand, some I have studied, and others I have researched. The people I have known who possess this aura of energy have inspired me to be my very best, have challenged me to reach higher, and have seen something inside me that I did not. Their behaviors, their actions, and their energy flipped a switch inside me that turned up my motivation to succeed.

By nature I am self-motivated, and yet these people and their effect made me supremely motivated.

Here you will learn the 10 steps you, as a leader, must take to create the powerful energy that will transform the organization around you. It is a process that is simple to understand, but like most skill development, more difficult to master. Each step in the 10-step process builds on the prior step.

Step 1. Remember the "who that you are." This first step is critical to the process. It begins inside you. You must do the important work necessary to identify, clarify, and confirm what is important to you first.

Step 2. Remove the shroud. Once you have *rediscovered* what is important to you, it is time to drum up the courage to commit to *act on* what is important to you.

Step 3. Study the legends and learn the folklore. After you understand your most important truths and have recommitted to acting on them, it's time to look outside yourself and to look back into your organization. Here we explain the importance of historical research. Who were the founders of your organization? What mattered to them? Why? What are the important stories that are folklore in your organization? What is important about them? You will learn how to apply what you glean from this new and different perspective, a historical one.

Step 4. Pay careful attention to the Alpha Dog. Next we look to the present, but again outside of ourselves. Who is the clear leader in your organization today? Who has authority *and* the ability to strongly influence others? To whom does everyone look for direction in difficult times? What matters to this person? Why? Are there others? Observing the actions of these important leaders in real time has great value to you. We will explain why.

Step 5. Query the key players. This step is about the truths within your organization as viewed by the people who matter most to it. What do they believe is important? Why? This is the critical "litmus test" that allows you to check what you have observed about yourself and key leaders historically and currently against the current beliefs of those others who are the peer leaders and are integral to the day-to-day operation of the organization. We will use a technique that builds trusted relations with your people as you learn the perspective of these important stakeholders.

Step 6. Crack the code to your "secret sauce." Here we explore a fascinating process for defining your culture's "secret sauce" in a way that will amplify the now resonating energy and leverage it to drive economic value into your business. You will focus your thinking on why your culture is different. What are the common threads that you now understand that make your organization special? If your organization seems to lack that "secret sauce," then we will help you figure out what the "missing ingredient" might be. This is a critical step to your being able to *broadcast* your powerful energy.

Step 7. Promote your resonating culture. Here you will learn to leverage your most important leadership tool, your communication ability. This step is about defining the message, capturing the story, and taking all that you've learned about yourself and your culture and putting it into a body of work that becomes a treasure trove of powerful words and phrases for you to tap into, on demand. This anthology holds the ingredients for amplifying the energy within you and within those around you.

Step 8. Create the Rally Cry. The most powerful messages are the simplest ones. However, simple is hard! Here you invest energy in refining your message and increasing its potency by simplifying it.

Step 9. Save the "saved." Speed is the key to success. To quickly realize the benefits from all your hard work, it's important to recognize the disciples who can take your message and spread the energy through your organization rapidly. To drive change and to move your organization in the direction you envision, you must identify and focus on these key people.

Step 10. Rise to your leadership best. The final step is ongoing because the economic climate changes rapidly. The process must be fluid and dynamic. Maximizing the energy within your culture requires you and the leaders around you to continually develop yourselves and become effective coaches to develop others. As a coach, you must constantly adapt to circumstances and flex, while remaining true to the core principles and beliefs you now understand. This is the key to effective "change leadership," an enormously important competence in business today.

Each step, it turns out, has at its core a principle. When you tap in to your own energy and follow these steps to *charge up* your organization, you and everyone impacted become powerful because you are tapping in to fundamental truths—*Providence moves too.*

> *There is one elementary truth the ignorance of which kills countless ideas and splendid plans: that the moment one definitely commits oneself, then Providence moves too.*
>
> —W. H. Murray, Scottish
> Mountaineer and Author

The entire process is captured in Figure I.1. The idea of this visual representation of the process is to fill time and space with your own innate and amplified energy. The relationship between time and space has been recognized as a significant physical principle since Einstein's theory of relativity was first published in 1905. By combining space and time, physicists, including Einstein, have been able to uncover the workings of the universe, leading to the release of previously unimaginably powerful energy—nuclear energy, for example. This book's chapters detail each step in the process that will allow you to release your own powerful energy.

FIGURE I.1 | THE ENERGY CONTINUUM

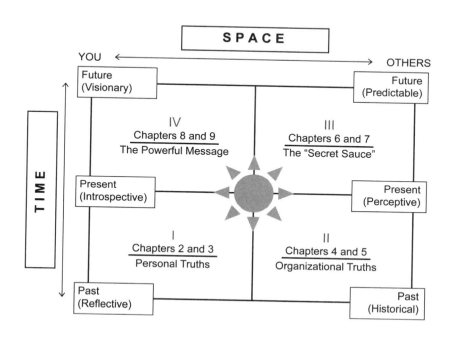

Starting with Quadrant I, your reflections on your past and self-introspection will help you determine your personal truths—the *who that you are*. Once you have gained key insights into your personal truths, we move to Quadrant II to an external perspective—organizational truths—again from both a historical and current perspective. In Quadrant III, we begin the work of tying together what you've learned. This is where resonance begins to have a profound effect. When the work in Quadrants I and II is done correctly, you begin to *feel* the energy as it is amplified inside you. Finally, in Quadrant IV you begin to define it. Here, you will use the only tool you have as a leader to propagate this energy, your communication skills. This is where your energy manifests itself in power! This diagram will serve as your road map throughout the process.

The exercises at the end of each chapter are cumulative, chapter to chapter. If you apply yourself fully, your fundamental truths as well as your organization's truths will emerge, and the two will merge, causing resonance. You will begin to feel a renewed sense of purpose as you clarify and recommit to acting on your personal truths. You will channel this energy through powerful communication that will energize others and move them to action. Finally, you will create an atmosphere of energy in your organization that will propel it forward faster and more successfully than you could have imagined. The power of resonance will help unleash the full potential of everyone around you and put your organization on the road to outstanding, distinctive, and unprecedented achievement.

READER BEWARE

There is a point in the process where the clarity of your purpose emerges so powerfully that there is no turning back. Like the airplane reaching critical speed on the runway, you *must* take off. Fear not. The people around you, your team, your department, your organization, your family and friends—indeed, those unknown many you will encounter in this world as you live your life—need the energy you have inside you. It will breathe life into those whose paths you cross, just as it does you.

In her book *A Return to Love: Reflections on the Principles of "A Course in Miracles,"* Marianne Williamson beautifully captured the essence of unleashing the energy inside you with this poignant assertion: "Our deepest fear is not that we are inadequate. Our deepest fear is that we are powerful beyond measure. It is our light, not our darkness, that most frightens us. We ask ourselves, Who am I to be brilliant, gorgeous, talented, and fabulous? Actually, who are you *not* to be? You are a child of God. Your playing small does not serve the world. There's nothing enlightened about shrinking so that other people won't feel insecure around you. We are all meant to shine, as children do. We were born to make manifest the glory of God that is within us. It's not just in some of us; it's in everyone. And as we let our own light shine, we unconsciously give other people permission to do the same. As we're liberated from our own fear, our presence automatically liberates others."

Once you've read this book, and have faithfully put the time and effort into the exercises, use the book as a reference tool. Later, you can reread the entire book, or you can go directly to the specific step you wish to focus on, refresh your understanding, and build on it. Remember, your *confidence* as a leader is a function of your *competence* as a leader. Your competence is a function of your skill. And your skills are learned behaviors acquired through study and practice. Each step in the process involves a skill you must develop.

Do the work and let the power of resonance do the rest!

The Power of Resonance

*Resonance is the effect produced when the natural vibration
frequency of a body is greatly amplified by reinforcing
vibrations at the same frequency from another body.*

—WEBSTER'S NEW WORLD DICTIONARY

There is something magical about hearing a symphony orchestra perform. Have you ever marveled at how a well-composed and well-played piece can penetrate your very soul? Although I am not a musician, past—and sometimes painful—endeavors to try to become one have given me an appreciation for music as well as for the enormous skill and practice required to play something pleasing to the ear.

Consider for a moment how multiple instruments, played well at the same time, create an effect that exceeds their additive value. The combination of sounds creates something so powerful that it engages the ear, yet finds its way to our soul and energizes our very emotional makeup. How does this happen?

Two musical instruments, a violin and a clarinet, help to shed light on this phenomenon. If the violin at any moment is playing a specific musical note, the sound it produces is related to the natural frequency of the note. If the clarinet plays the exact same note with the corresponding same frequency, the resulting sound will perfectly synchronize the two sources, providing a pleasing example of resonance. Extrapolate this to an entire orchestra playing a symphony, and resonance plays a major role in the sound and effect it produces. It is important, of course, to recognize that the pleasing effect of resonating instruments is greatly enhanced by the genius of the conductor, the composition of the score, and the talent of the musicians playing the instruments. If we apply this orchestral analogy to a business organization, the conductor equates to the CEO, the composition of the score to the business strategy, and the musicians themselves to the people in the organization charged with the responsibility of executing the business strategy.

When the economic crisis struck the United States in 2008, I was one of many executives who wondered how my company would weather the challenge. At the time, I was the senior vice president of human resources for Raymour & Flanigan, a rapidly growing giant in the retail furniture industry.

From an outsider's perspective, it probably looked bad for us. While everyone needs furniture, it's not as if we were selling food or medicine. Furniture is a classic discretionary purchase. With consumer confidence plummeting along with the Dow Jones Industrial Average, it would have been understandable if our organization suffered through this era as well.

That never happened. Despite the fact that we worked in a languishing industry and faced the most challenging economic conditions since the Great Depression, we marched forward with our quest to grow the business from $250 million to $1 billion in sales. We continued to gobble up market share in every major city we moved into, including Philadelphia and New York. Perhaps most impressively, we had lenders clamoring to provide us with capital at a time when debt financing in our industry was basically nonexistent. Confronting our greatest moment of truth as a leadership team, we remained united in moving toward our common goal. We wanted to make the company the best retail furniture company in the country, and we never wavered despite the adversity.

In addition to being a career highlight for me, this turned out to be a profound learning experience. How did we do it? As I sift through my memories of those days like a California gold rush miner, two precious nuggets stand out: *leadership and energy*. And you can't have one without the other.

We had several great leaders in our fast-growing retail furniture organization. At the top of the list was Neil Goldberg, the CEO and my boss. From the moment I met him, I sensed that there was something special about him. His reputation as a gifted business leader preceded our first meeting, but as I got to know Neil, it was clear that his talents and his character were understated. Although Neil was extremely humble and eschewed public recognition, an aura of energy radiated from him.

Neil's energy proved to be contagious. Its dynamic force affected all aspects of the business. It inspired our logistics experts to reinvent their spoke-and-wheel model, resulting in enormous cost savings. It pushed our sales and marketing gurus to keep consumers coming into our stores when they had plenty of justification to stay home. In my area, the infectious energy resulted in the creation of a Leadership Development Institute that ultimately helped us bottle the secret sauce of our success and use it to drive our leaders' values from headquarters into every storefront across the company.

We celebrated our successes, but this vital energy also kept us hungry. We were winners on a winning team, but our Rally Cry was "Raise the Bar," as our passion was to see how much better we could be as a company. Neil's energy permeated our own, aligned us, and amplified through us, creating an energized culture.

Neil had a giant photo of basketball legend Michael Jordan, palming a basketball with each hand, hanging in his office. If you were a new executive leader at Raymour & Flanigan and were important enough to have a seat at Neil Goldberg's table, he'd say, "You know why I have that up there?"

And people would say, "Sure. It's because Jordan was the icon of being the best. He's a winner."

"It's not just that," Neil would say. "It's because every time he walked on to the basketball court, he raised everybody's game around him . . . whether he was feeling 100 percent or 50 percent. Didn't matter. Everybody played better around Michael Jordan, and that's what leadership is all about."

And Neil consistently lived up to those words. I remember one time: It was before the recession, but there were major economic issues brewing that led to many failures in the furniture industry. The Mom and

Pop stores no longer had the critical mass. The big nationals were run by financiers who were driven by numbers. They were out of touch with what customers really wanted.

Over the previous two years, we had already doubled our revenues from roughly $250 million to about $500 million. Anybody would be happy with that. Well, Neil assembled the executive leadership team at a bar in Connecticut and said, "I want to penetrate metropolitan New York."

It was a crazy idea. It was the middle of the recession, and we're going into the most competitive market there is? We were exhausted. We all looked at each other. One bold colleague was brave enough to say, "Neil, have you thought about this?"

Now, Neil's style was to listen. What were the risks? Why wouldn't we do this? So from each of our perspectives, we all explained what the risks were. For my part, I told him our human resources were already spread too thin. We didn't have the bench strength, and I wasn't sure the culture that had made us successful outside of metro New York would work its wonders within metro New York. My assumption turned out to be wrong, which taught me a great deal about what can be overcome when you're working in a high-energy culture.

Neil heard everyone out. Then he smiled, looked down at his drink, and said, "I appreciate all your opinions, and I respect every one of you . . . but we're going in."

So after three scotches, I walked out of the bar. And despite the drinks, I remember very clearly thinking, "Man this is nuts . . . but all right . . . *bring it on!*"

Neil Goldberg was successful because he raised the game of everyone around him. That's a core definition of what great leaders do to energize their teams. Neil was not afraid of taking risks. He knew that you can only take risks of that scope if you're surrounded by the right people and if you're the kind of leader who raises everybody's game. Neil Goldberg was that kind of leader.

Now I look back and marvel at how we overcame such overwhelming odds and reached $1 billion in sales—"we happy few" as Shakespeare's Henry V said while reflecting with his small band of vastly outnumbered underdogs after they defied the odds to defeat the French in the Battle of Agincourt.

A TWENTY-FIRST-CENTURY ENERGY CRISIS

When I became the president of Bates Communications in 2010, I embarked on a series of conversations with executives from great organizations across the country. Frequently, I heard of companies at which individuals had risen in the ranks due to their technical brilliance and impressive individual accomplishments. Now, though, they had reached a point in their careers where their technical skills had taken them as far as they could go. At this crossroads, they needed to be transformed into powerful leaders who could inspire people, energize their culture, and get results.

Many organizations now face what I would describe as a twenty-first-century "energy crisis." The one I'm referring to has nothing to do with the price of oil, though. While the economy has bounced back to some degree, many leadership challenges have become magnified and elevated in importance, particularly as workforces have been trimmed to the bone and leaders taxed to their limits. A major one is in the area of employee engagement.

Employee engagement is not the same as job satisfaction. According to Scarlett Surveys, "Employee engagement is a measureable degree of an employee's positive or negative emotional attachment to their job, colleagues and organization which profoundly influences their willingness to learn and perform at work." Engaged employees truly care about the company and feel a connection to it. As a result, they are willing to invest the energy to be great instead of having the attitude that it's "good enough to be good enough."

Gallup conducts research on employee engagement, asking 12 questions revolving around employee perceptions. Here are the themes that the questions cover:

▸ Having clear expectations and everything needed to do the best job every day

▸ Feeling that leadership cares about employees as people and is interested in their professional development

▸ Getting recognized for good performance

▶ Having a voice

▶ Feeling a sense of purpose

▶ Working among people who want to do quality work

So how are we doing as a nation with employee engagement? Consider this startling data from a September 2010 Gallup poll:

▶ At *world-class* organizations, the ratio of engaged to disengaged employees was roughly *10 to 1*.

▶ At *average* organizations, that ratio was just about *2 to 1*.

▶ Disengaged employees cost U.S. companies roughly $800 billion in productivity annually.

▶ Engaged organizations have 3.9 times the earnings-per-share growth rate compared with that of organizations with lower engagement in their same industry.

The accompanying report noted that "the best-performing companies know that an employee engagement improvement strategy linked to the achievement of corporate goals will help them win in the marketplace." So creating a high-energy culture is not just a feel-good enterprise. It's a crucial differentiator between the best companies and those that are average . . . or worse.

CREATING A HIGH-ENERGY CULTURE

One of the challenges in leading the high-energy culture is that an organization's energy is not always easy to assess. Sometimes energy is like a mirage in the desert: From a distance, it seems to be there, only to dissolve upon closer inspection. At other times, an organization is more like a beehive: From the outside, it seems like not much is happening, but look inside and you'll see a stunning display of interdependent roles and purpose-driven behavior.

According to the laws of physics, energy can never be created or destroyed. It can build up in one place and dissipate in another. It can be a productive or destructive force. Music is but one example of the importance and power of resonating energy. It provides insight into the natural order of energy transmission that applies to the way a high-energy culture works. High-energy cultures are those in which the leaders reinforce the natural vibration frequency of the people in the organization. As a leader, you must understand the power of resonance if you are to create a high-energy culture. Like the conductor of the symphony orchestra, it is incumbent on you as a leader to act in a way that synchronizes the rhythms of your associates and amplifies the frequency of their natural vibrations.

In one sense, organizational energy is like a loose live wire: If you handle it carefully and plug it in appropriately, it's a source of power. Mishandle it, and you'll receive a painful jolt!

On the other hand, nature demonstrates that powerful occurrences are not necessarily a function of brute force. A simple, common example of this is a child pushing another child on a swing. Much like a pendulum, a swing has a natural frequency of oscillating motion. The natural frequency (the number of complete cycles back and forth in a given time interval) is directly related to the length of the swing. However, the height the swing reaches at the endpoint of each back-and-forth movement is directly related to the timing of the force applied to the swing. Thus, if a very strong adult pushes the swing at a random frequency to the natural cycle of the swing, the swing varies in the height it achieves. But if a child pushes the same swing with a frequency equal to the natural frequency of the swing, thus achieving resonance, the height, or amplitude, increases greatly. At resonance, relatively little effort is necessary to obtain a greater height. A child pushing a swing in sync with the natural frequency of the arc can cause the swing to go higher than can a full-grown muscular adult pushing a similar swing out of sync with its natural frequency.

As I reflect on the leaders I've known personally—as well as those that I've researched for this book—one common trait is that all of them have earned an on-the-job Ph.D. in what we could call "organizational energy." They seemed to know the exact force and timing to "push the swing" that is their organization. They create an atmosphere where their employees flourish, and their words and actions have an energy that resonates with everyone that they encounter. Why should you, as a successful leader, consider the importance of resonance as you plan and decide how you will drive increasing value into your organization? How does creating a high-energy culture in your organization translate into economic returns?

> *Energy and persistence conquer all things.*
> —BENJAMIN FRANKLIN, AMERICAN
> PATRIOT, DIPLOMAT, AND INVENTOR

A DIAMOND ENGAGEMENT RING

Great leaders recognize the power of their resonating energy, and they have the courage to act on an irrepressible desire inside of themselves. As a result, in our era of disengagement, these traits make them valuable commodities. Unfortunately, they are very rare commodities, too. Why?

It's not because only a few people are blessed with a certain gift that others simply do not possess. Quite the contrary: My own experience as a successful business leader, as a student of leadership, and as a coach who has helped develop leaders with enormously powerful and economically valuable intrinsic energy refutes that. The work we did in the Leadership Development Institute we created—where we researched, studied, identified, clarified, and mapped the steps necessary to spawn this energy within other leaders and within an organization—absolutely proves that armed with the knowledge, clarity of purpose, and commitment to become the best, you possess this capability.

> *My experience has convinced me that anyone dedicated is capable of becoming a truly great leader because each of us has this potential inside.*

I don't just mean those leaders with an impressive job title. I'm talking about being any leader who:

▸ Energizes those around her through making her internal energy contagious

- Communicates clearly, with purpose and passion
- Behaves consistent with her own personal beliefs and values

When this energy is focused and transferred through powerful communication, the organization around this type of leader becomes powerfully charged. This translates into real economic value in the form of steep growth, market-share dominance, and benchmark bottom-line results.

Leaders who possess this energizing quality are rare only because few people understand how to *tap* the power of the energy that already exists within them and how to use it to inspire and invigorate those they lead: their teams, their department, and their entire organization. This atmosphere of energy that bonds an impassioned, authentic leader and those who choose to follow her is what I call the *high-energy culture*.

To put it another way, every organization has a healthy number of unpolished diamonds in its ranks. At a glance, these diamonds don't yet have what it takes to sparkle and shine as leaders. But with time, effort, education, patience, and persistence, it's possible to polish these rough gems and place them in the right setting—some place where anyone can see their allure and value. And when you have an organization loaded with diamonds, imagine the impact! And by the way, a diamond is always a good sign of engagement.

A Prerequisite for the High-Energy Culture

While we absolutely can turn rough diamonds into polished gems, no organization can turn a hunk of coal into a diamond. That's not necessarily an impossible feat, but it requires more time, patience, and resources than most organizations are willing to or can afford to invest.

Great leaders have an enormous impact because they tap into the same truths in others that motivate them. Research, experience, and intuition all support the proposition that organizations flourish on the overt, collective *self-motivation* of each individual. Jim Collins, leadership researcher and author of *Built to Last* and *Good to Great*, explains the relationship between companies that are ultra successful and the significance of motivation. "[Companies that make the change from good to great] don't motivate people—their people are self-motivated."

Collins postulates that the most important thing a leader can do is to get the "right people on the bus." Underlying this is the principle that all greatness within companies begins and ends with people. The key question is not what motivates people; rather, it is what "self-motivates" people.

For decades, behaviorists maintained that motivation was externally influenced, using rewards as stimuli. Picture the mouse that learns to press a bar in a cage to receive a food pellet. However, humans aren't so simple. More recently, pioneer psychologists such as Edward Deci and Richard Ryan have begun to reject this long-held belief through their research in the area of self-determination theory (SDT). SDT holds that "motivation develops inside us, and is grounded in our basic human need to develop our own skills and capacities, to act of our own accord (freedom), and *to connect others and our environment.*" This motivation is called *intrinsic motivation.*

Basically, Deci and Ryan are saying that intrinsic motivation is the drive to do something because it is interesting and satisfying in itself. However, the theory also states that to reach their full potential, people need nurturing from the social environment.

Leadership author Stephen Covey has long held that reaching their full potential is the ultimate goal of all humans. He maintains that, as humans, we have four dimensions: the heart, the mind, the body, and the spirit. In order to feel fulfilled and find true meaning in life, we need to explore and expand ourselves in each of these four dimensions. All of us have the capacity to expand our inherent talents and capabilities, and given the right nurturing, have the intrinsic motivation to do so.

RESONANCE: SOME GET IT AND OTHERS DON'T

Leaders must lead in a way that resonates socially with the intrinsic motivation of their people. Yet those people have to come to the organization with a reasonable degree of self-motivation. Both aspects are key to creating a high-energy culture.

LEADERS WHO GET IT

Leaders who understand the power of this social resonance may be rare, but they are fascinating in their variety. When we think of CEOs who lead a high-energy culture, several widely recognized names quickly come to mind. Look at the late Steve Jobs and how integral his role was in making Apple a top global brand with its own unique culture. More recently, Alan Mulally of the Ford Motor Company is an inspiring story. Mulally's energy turned around a company that was losing $14 billion a year. As we'll see in examples later in this book, it wasn't magic. It was all about choosing the behaviors and words that would convince his people that they could be as great as the company had been back in the heyday of Henry Ford in the 1920s.

However, you don't have to rise in the corporate ranks like Mulally to lead a high-energy culture. Take, for instance, Kathy Ireland, a former high-profile fashion model. After her ultra successful career as a model came to an end, she felt empty in terms of personal fulfillment. With no experience in the field, but with an inner sense of initiative and drive, she founded a high-energy, multibillion-dollar company, Kathy Ireland Home. The company is dedicated to helping women have everything they want in spite of the hectic nature of their lives and even with all the competing demands on their time. In 2006, *Forbes* declared her to be the "prototype for the model-turned-mogul." She now pulls in an estimated $10 million per year.

And yet her humility is startling. In an interview with Parents TV in 2009, Ireland said, "I always knew I belonged on the other side of the camera. I'm grateful for that career back in the last century, did okay, but certainly wasn't 'super.' . . . I tried and failed at many businesses before starting our own brand in 1993 with a pair of socks. It was a big celebration when we sold our 100 millionth pair. I was so grateful to the women out there who turned down the noise of stereotyping and embraced our brand.

"I tell people I have the toughest boss in the world, and I love her: It's the moms out there. Our mission statement is finding solutions for families—especially busy moms."

In January 2009, I saw Kathy deliver a keynote address to our high-achieving associates at an event at my company. From her presentation and presence at the event, everyone could feel the depth and sincerity of her commitment to her personal truths. Her passion and leadership style were so compelling, you could see them reflected in the eyes of the audience, most profoundly in the eyes of the women attending. That power of her commitment to her personal truths and her business associates discounted any preconceived notion that her brand was all about "a pretty face and swimsuit body." Consistent with Covey's mantra of unleashing the full potential of those all around you, Ireland shared her compelling purpose of helping working mothers succeed in being whole people, successful in all roles that working mothers play, for their children, their partner, their family, and their business. Her speech resonated universally with everyone in the room.

Some leaders who get it are not in the corporate ranks at all. California schoolteacher Rafe Esquith mostly teaches poor kids who often are the children of immigrants. Due to the high-energy culture he's created, his students often arrive voluntarily at 6:30 a.m., two hours before school officially starts. They stay as late as 6 p.m. and willingly come in during weekends and holidays. In the documentary *The Hobart Shakespeareans*, it's impossible to remain dry eyed as you watch these fourth graders skip recess to learn to play guitar, sob because they are so moved by reading *Huckleberry Finn* aloud, and put on a brilliant production of a Shakespeare play. It's a profound example of people's tendency to rise (or sink) to the level of expectations that have been set for them.

If you sift for gold as you reflect on your own personal experiences, you're almost sure to think of remarkable individuals who were able to energize you from your past. They may have been coaches or parents just as easily as they were managers or mentors. As this book progresses, I'll share stories about energizing leaders and ask you to dig into your own experiences—your own stories—as well. Studying powerful stories is key in our quest to learning fundamental truths, both personal and organizational. Stories are windows that allow us to see truths so that we can clarify them and act on them. Identifying and clarifying truths are primal to creating social resonance and leading a high-energy culture.

COMPANIES THAT GET IT

Today more than ever, businesses need to understand the significance of social resonance as a necessary component of their culture if they're going to succeed at the highest level of their potential—as determined by their business model. Businesses without a culture of social resonance may succeed, be profitable, and achieve a level of success. However, without a culture of social resonance, these businesses will never reach a sustained, high level of performance regardless of market conditions, nor will they have the *attractive power* to consistently obtain the very best customers and employees.

People yearn for meaning in their lives, and they flourish when participating in an organization that both connects with what's in their hearts and souls and aligns with their personal truths. To feel that critical sense of engagement at work, people need to have a sense of mission and purpose beyond just completing a task because they are directed to do so.

This hierarchy of human needs was poignantly described by Jim Kouzes and Barry Posner in the preface to the third edition of their enormously popular book *The Leadership Challenge*. Nearly 20 years after the book's first publication, Kouzes and Posner wondered whether their five practices of leadership were still valid. These are the five practices:

- Leaders model the way.

- Leaders inspire a shared vision.

- Leaders enable others to act.

- Leaders challenge the process.

- Leaders encourage the heart.

Following up on their original theory, they asked current leaders, "What's new, and what's different?" Studying the responses, they found that people in organizations now have an "even more intense search for meaning."

The authors wrote: "In the last half-decade a countervailing force has arisen to combat what seemed to be an ever-expanding sense of cynicism. Younger workers aren't giving in to the idea that they don't make a difference. Aging baby boomers are back to exploring their souls. More and more of us are on a quest for greater meaning in our lives. Whether you call it spirituality, religion, faith, or soul, there's clearly a trend toward a greater openness to the spiritual side within the walls of business. Values and virtues are discussed more openly, and people worry about the legacy they're leaving."

The book *Firms of Endearment: How World-Class Companies Profit from Passion and Purpose,* by Raj Sisodia, David B. Wolfe, and Jag Sheth, draws a similar parallel. The authors discuss "deep-seated changes in how people see things in mainstream business culture. Consider the words *affection, love, joy, authenticity, empathy, compassion, soulfulness* and other terms of endearment. Until recently, such words had no place in business. However, that is changing. Today, a growing number of companies . . . comfortably embrace such terms. That is why we coined the phrase *firms of endearment.* Quite simply, an FOE (firm of endearment) is a company that *endears* itself to stakeholders by bringing the interests of all stakeholder groups into strategic alignment."

Sisodia, Wolfe, and Sheth argue that "endearing companies tend to be enduring companies" and share "a distinctive set of core values, policies, and operating attributes." In other words, they resonate socially.

The authors identify companies they believe meet these social resonance criteria. Among them is Whole Foods, which captures social resonance in its formal Declaration of Interdependence that "acknowledges the idea that stakeholder groups constitute a family whose members depend on one another." In its declaration, Whole Foods states: "Our motto—Whole Foods, Whole People, Whole Planet—emphasizes that our vision reaches far beyond just being a food retailer. Our success in fulfilling our vision is measured by customer satisfaction, Team Member excellence and happiness . . . and local and larger community support."

Later in that same document, the company says: "One of the most important responsibilities of Whole Foods Market's leadership is to make sure the interests, desires, and needs of our various stakeholders are kept in balance. We recognize that this is a dynamic process. It requires participation and communication by all of our stakeholders. It requires listening compassionately, thinking carefully and acting with integrity . . .

Creating and nurturing this community of stakeholders is critical to the long-term success of the company." Clearly, Whole Foods understands and practices social resonance.

Another "firm of endearment" identified by Sisodia, Wolfe, and Sheth is Patagonia, a company that makes a conscious effort to hire people who are passionate about the company and its products, much as Collins proposed as having the "right people on the bus." Patagonia makes a concerted effort to align the interests of its employees with those of the larger corporate philosophy, a reflection of its core values. Patagonia focuses its employment efforts on people who have a passion for the environment and mountain climbing. More important, it "walks the talk" by giving time to its employees to enjoy outdoor and environmental activities. In doing so, it is encouraging and fostering a culture of social resonance throughout the company, and as a result, it is enhancing the commitment of its employees to success and productivity.

The impact of Patagonia's culture reaches beyond the company to its suppliers. Patagonia insists on commitment to environmental standards and social responsibility from its vendors. While implementing the consequent need to retool their production processes, these suppliers have experienced higher productivity and profits—testament to the pervasive impact of social resonance.

A corporate behemoth such as Google encourages innovation by allowing employees to spend one day per week working on the project of their choice. Atlassian Software—a small software developer—has occasional "FedEx Days" in which a new idea has to be created, developed, and delivered absolutely, positively overnight—with a pizza party at the end of the day to celebrate the winners. Regardless of the organization's size, companies that get it aren't afraid to do something different that captures the core values and truths of their leaders.

PUT ON YOUR OWN OXYGEN MASK FIRST

The question now: Where should you begin? The underlying principle of resonating leadership is that each of us is a potentially powerful source of energy. Your goal is to create an atmosphere within your organization that:

▶ Promotes self-motivation within its people

▶ Attracts capital resources (both human and financial)

▶ Creates synergy

▶ Synchronizes all stakeholders to generate enormous economic value

Natural frequencies occur everywhere, from the earth's 24-hour rotation and the moon's regular frequency of revolution around the earth on a macro scale, to consistently vibrating atoms in an atomic clock (the underlying purpose for their use in a universal standards clock) on a micro scale.

There is evidence in nature that bodies of the same natural frequencies tend to want to synchronize. In order to synchronize all your stakeholders and to marshal their collective action to drive enormous economic value, you must tap the energy within yourself first. Think of the instructions you receive as you fasten your seat belt and prepare for departure on a flight: "Put on your own oxygen mask before assisting others." As a leader, you need to start by focusing more than you ever have before on the wellspring of your own energy. You will become more authentic, more personally satisfied, and more effective when your thoughts and actions are in tune with your own natural frequency.

So from a personal development perspective, what is required?

The single most important factor is *clarity of personal truths*. Why this is so imperative is thoroughly explained in the next chapter. And like most principles, this one seems simple on the surface. It's not. It's hard work. It takes commitment, effort, and patience, and it begins with intense reflection. Throughout this book, I'll ask you to reflect on people in your life who were important to your growth and development. Identifying these people is a key factor in your continued development as a leader. It is essential for being able to tap the energy within you. The first step in the process ahead is to look back into your past. As the reflection process unfolds, you will be surprised to learn of the extraordinary power that lies latent within you. So fasten your seat belt, take a deep breath from your oxygen mask, and turn to the exercise that follows this page.

Sifting for Gold

REFLECT ON YOUR DEEPEST BELIEFS

Consumed by the hectic pace of life today, each of us may have forgotten the important beliefs deep inside us. When we focus on those things that are most important to us, we find that they often originated early in our lives. We may have learned them through observation and meaningful conversations with our parents, guardians, friends, teachers, coaches, or religious leaders. In some instances, we may have learned them through serendipitous interactions with acquaintances that otherwise had no significant impact on our growth and development: They just happened to be in the right place at the right time, and they had an indelible impact upon us.

This activity requires your commitment of time for reflection. You're not just gazing at your navel! You're sifting for gold, and those precious nuggets might not be the first that come to mind. This can't be done in five minutes. Be patient. I highly recommend that you commit a minimum of 30 minutes and that you do so in an environment devoid of distraction—always a challenge in this digital age.

In the left column in the worksheet for this exercise, list what you believe are your most important and deepest beliefs. These could range from very individual values, such as statements about family, spirituality, love, respect for others, wealth, learning, and personal achievement, to more global values, such as democracy, freedom, justice, and global welfare. Don't hurry through this aspect of the activity. Take your time, because this activity could have a significant and permanent impact on the remainder of your life. When you clarify and understand your deepest beliefs, decisions are suddenly easier to make. You can let go of those protracted internal debates about which choice is the right choice; your beliefs dictate the right choice.

What if you have no idea of where to start when it comes to capturing some of your possible personal truths? Here are some questions that might help you think of themes:

- ▸ Think of times that you have found yourself bursting with energy. What specific activities triggered that feeling?

- ▸ Reflect on past situations where you sensed that something was missing. What was it?

- ▸ Consider a few defining moments in your career, whether they were great accomplishments or significant setbacks. What did you learn about what was important to you in the process?

- ▸ When you've talked with close friends or family over the last six months, what stories are you most eager to share? What are those stories really *about* if you think about the themes, lessons, and values they convey?

- ▸ Think of the best leaders you've known over the years, whether they were in an office, classroom, or some other setting. What did those leaders stand for? What values did they espouse in their words and deeds that energized you deeply?

Once you have completed the list, think deeply about how you acquired each value or belief if you haven't done so already. Was it from one of your parents or guardians? Was it from a friend whom you haven't spoken to for 20 years? Was it from a teacher or coach? Maybe it was part of a passing conversation with a business acquaintance. Was it from a complete stranger, like someone who stopped along the road to help you with your disabled vehicle?

Last, for each value and source you have identified, take several minutes to ponder the profundity of both. Consider how both have influenced your life.

Reflections on My Personal Truths and Deepest Beliefs

Personal Truths and Deepest Beliefs	Source
Example: *Real* learning is a major investment, but it pays lifelong dividends	Example: Mr. Grover's eleventh-grade Term Paper class

2

Remember the "Who That You Are"

That we should know ourselves means that we should know our souls.

—SOCRATES, GREEK PHILOSOPHER

Ra'ad Siraj, currently the managing director and chief technology officer of The Boston Company Asset Management, grew up as the son of a Saudi Arabian diplomat. As a result, his family raised him in a variety of countries—Lebanon, Egypt, Italy, Switzerland, and England as well as Saudi Arabia—each with its own language, culture, and values (much like every organization). When living in Saudi Arabia, he was struck by how different the experience was from what he experienced in other nations. "There was no feeling of being in control," he says. "There was a sense that you exist at the whim of those in power."

While back in Saudi Arabia at one time, Siraj recalls going to see his father at his office with some minor grievance that he wanted to air. Having spent many years at an American school in Rome, Siraj had grown accustomed to the American style of being straightforward and cutting to the chase. So he did exactly that in his father's office with ambassadors from other countries present, ignoring the local protocol of a strict series of steps that one must follow in a scenario like that. That night, Siraj's father made it very clear that, while he loved him very much, (a) that was not the way to handle the situation, given the local values, and (b) his concern would've been addressed if he simply had adhered to the protocol that was needed at that office with ambassadors present.

These experiences had a profound impact on him as a child. From watching his father's role as a diplomat, he learned how valuable it was to be able to adapt and quickly read the lay of the land and create trusted relationships. He discovered that you could change your behaviors to fit in with local customs . . . without compromising your personal integrity. From living under the monarchy in Saudi Arabia, he came to understand that people need to have a stake in what they're doing. "It's like the quote from Thomas Friedman and Larry Summers about renting a car versus owning one," he says. "You're going to take much better care of something if you have a sense of ownership."

Early in his career, Siraj worked for Arthur D. Little as a management consultant. To be successful in that field, he needed to embrace a big-picture view of business issues rather than a narrow focus on technology. He also needed to have a strong focus on communication and client satisfaction.

All these experiences have shaped who he has become as a chief information and technology officer. His deep-seated belief in creating trusted relationships as well as his consulting background has led to his belief that "there is no such thing as an IT issue, only business issues with IT components." His early experiences in different countries have helped him adapt as he has changed industries as a business leader. Much of that adaptability goes back to his father's lesson: "You get more cooperation when you attempt to speak the local language," whether literally or figuratively.

Now that you've begun to reflect on your deepest beliefs, journeying back to the past to do so, it's important to note that *today is a new day*. The journey that you have undertaken will set you on a course that will undoubtedly help you reach your full potential as a leader.

Like any journey, this one begins with a single step. The journey to remember the "who that you are," perhaps for the first time, begins today. I know this sounds counterintuitive. How can you "remember" something for the first time? You've experienced life; you simply may have forgotten how the stories of your life have shaped you. If you think of life as a series of experiences, many of which have contributed to shaping who you are, then you'll get a glimpse of what I mean by "remember who you are for the first time." Your significant life stories, it turns out, will be enormously important to your success as a leader as we move through the process of clarifying your personal truths to create effective high-energy leadership.

In the last chapter, we used the analogy of putting on your oxygen mask first before attempting to assist others. Leaders need to be very clear on what made them who they are before they can attempt to influence and inspire others. Why is that? To fully appreciate it, let's take a deeper look at the nature of energy.

THE NATURE OF RESONATING ENERGY

When we see a powerful speaker, listen to waves crashing at the seashore, or watch a great film like *The King's Speech,* something happens inside of us. In different ways, these experiences *resonate* with us. Quite literally, this means that we have a "natural vibration frequency" in our bodies and that an outside force has *amplified* that frequency by reinforcing vibrations at the same frequency. So when we say that we're on the "same wavelength" as someone, it could be literally true!

This phenomenon is not limited to the effect that people have on each other. When an opera singer can shatter a crystal goblet by singing a note of just the right frequency at full voice, the same thing is happening. The goblet has its own natural vibration frequency, and the sound waves emitted by the voice amplify that frequency—so much so that the glass shatters.

How about tuning forks? If two tuning forks are close enough together, the striking of one, putting it in motion, will cause the other to vibrate, whereas it originally had been still. The resulting energy increase of the second is observable, real, and predictable. Without the first, the second would remain idle—a truly demonstrable example of one body's energy impacting and intensifying the energy of a second.

The lesson is simple: Energy is a powerful force that can be amplified greatly . . . but only if the energy provider is in sync with and on the same wavelength as the recipient of that energy, allowing us to amplify its effect. So what exactly *intensifies* the energy within us, whatever its cause?

The answer is our own *personal truths,* or PTs. The vibrating energy inside us is amplified when we are clear on and act consistently with our PTs. To lead a high-energy culture, you need to emit vibrating energy on the right wavelength. You can't make your team reach greater heights by pushing that swing at a random moment. You need to start by looking within to determine your own natural frequency. That's entirely possible . . . but not as easy as it sounds!

BEACONS AND BUOYS

Life is a series of experiences, and it is ephemeral. Now, with the sophistication of technology, the speed at which our lives seem to be moving is increasing exponentially. Every day we are barraged with dozens of e-mails, phone calls, tweets, memos, and conversations. We live in the Age of Distraction. It's become increasingly difficult to wade through all the noise to find the signal.

In a sense, we're all like ships sailing on turbulent seas in foggy conditions. We get so caught up in trying to react to the waves that we forget to keep any eye out for the beacons that are always on solid ground, guiding us from a distant lighthouse. We forget the fact that we also have buoys that are there to show us the way and keep us afloat. These buoys and beacons are constants on a sea of change—for you and for those whom you lead. Kouzes and Posner state, "When sailing through the turbulent seas of change and uncertainty the crew needs a vision of what lies beyond the horizon, and they also must understand the standards by which performance will be judged."

Many of the executives we coach lament the fact that in their quest to become increasingly successful, they are moving further and further away from what's truly important to them. Does this sound familiar? We're moving rapidly from one task to the next, doing whatever is necessary to achieve whatever we seek. We stop looking for those buoys and beacons, or we take them for granted. The speed of our lives often prevents us from taking time to reflect.

Wouldn't it be wonderful if we could simplify our lives, slow down, and be more effective? Identifying—or rediscovering—your buoys and beacons will make life simpler for you.

When you have true clarity on where you've been and
where you're going, you won't waste valuable energy going
in the wrong directions.

THE IMPERATIVE OF INTROSPECTION

As you seek buoys and beacons amid the clouds of tasks and duties, you won't find them magically. It begins with introspection. This is the intentional, purposeful process of reporting to yourself your inner thoughts, feelings, paradigms, and desires. It requires commitment on your part to set aside time, free from distraction, to probe within your consciousness the foundations of your decisions, actions, and behaviors. It should be regular and genuine.

Regular and purposeful introspection helps ensure that our actions and behaviors are consistent with our fundamental selves, our personal truths, and serves to bolster self-confidence and self-assurance and the vibrating frequency of our own energy.

As leaders, we regularly analyze and assess the actions and behaviors of others. Sometimes we do so consciously and sometimes subconsciously. It's a natural and essential component of your role as leader. However, just as others' actions and behaviors are clues to what is meaningful and important to them, our actions and behaviors are clues for others about what is important to us. Thus, to be most effective as a leader you must focus not only on the actions and behaviors of others but also on your own actions and behaviors.

It is important to periodically delve into the roots of your consciousness to try to understand the basis of your thinking, your feelings, your desires, your paradigms, and your biases. Given the importance of self-assurance to effective leadership, we tend to push reflection aside. We don't have time for it! Yet from an organizational perspective, what could be more important than the leader's periodic self-reflection to ensure that his thoughts, actions, and behaviors are consistent with his innermost beliefs and their associated biases?

In their book, *Hard Facts, Dangerous Half-Truths, and Total Nonsense*, organizational management authors Jeffrey Pfeffer and Robert

Sutton share this perspective: "Because leaders succumb to the same self-enhancement as everyone else, magnified by the adulation they receive, they have a tendency to lose their behavioral inhibitions and behave in destructive ways. They need to avoid this trap and maintain an attitude of wisdom and a healthy dose of modesty."

The bottom line is that periodic introspection as a purposeful process is an important and necessary activity for us as leaders because it keeps us centered, energized, and balanced.

THE STORY OF YOUR LIFE

The journey to define your personal truths, perhaps for the first time, begins today. This is easy in theory and difficult in practice, but why? Recent research on a learning theory called *metacognition* shows us why. Metacognition is "knowing about knowing." Incredibly, research shows that most people don't really "know what they know." We all possess a locked treasure chest of experiences, but all too often we leave it locked. The ability to transfer knowledge in this way is like a muscle that we all have but that we don't often work to strengthen. So one key to defining your personal truths is making yourself more aware of your past thoughts and behaviors, as this will help you tap in to them as you adapt to new situations. This level of awareness and adaptability in our changing environments is very important to your development as a leader.

If you're like most people, you simply may have forgotten how the stories of your life have shaped you as a person and as a leader. Your significant life stories, it turns out, will be enormously important to your success as a leader as we move through the process of clarifying your personal truths to create effective high-energy leadership.

FROM PERSONAL STORIES TO PERSONAL TRUTHS

Later in the book, I'll share several stories that will illuminate how great CEOs lead the high-energy culture. For now, though, let's focus on the connection from personal stories to personal truths.

I don't want to play a semantics game here, but there is an important reason why I differentiate between *personal truths* and *values*. The power of personal truths goes well beyond identifying them. They reside in your resolve to actively confirm them, commit to them, and act on them.

Many words become so overused that they ultimately lose their meaning. *Integrity* is a perfect example. Kouzes and Posner's research on this indicated that the word *integrity* could have 185 different definitions based on the responses they received when asking thousands of people to define the word. I believe *values* has suffered a similar fate, and thus I will use the term *personal truths* to represent the critical concept you will need to understand here.

Personal truths are similar to one of the many definitions of values. They are shaped by your experiences as well as by an innate force inside you. *Personal truths* is a good descriptor because they are just what the term implies—they are *personal* because they are uniquely yours, and they are *truths* because they are a fundamental part of who you are. Other people may have similar PTs, and, in fact, the high-energy culture is a direct result of common PTs, but first things first.

Once personal truths are defined and clarified, they give us the potential to create powerful energy within us and others. Just like the child being pushed on the swing, our personal truths are the force that amplifies the natural frequency of the vibrations inside us. When we act in concert with these truths, our personal and professional success surges higher and higher, like the arc of the swing. Defining and clarifying your personal truths as a leader is the precursor to the high-energy culture.

Becoming a great leader is a function of your own personal truths, and to know these truths you must make time to reflect on and understand them. In his book *Drive*, Daniel Pink emphasizes the significance of personal reflection. He believes in the importance of searching deep inside yourself to come to grips with your bottom-line, focused personal goal.

Pink cites Clare Boothe Luce, the first woman elected to the U.S. Congress, who encouraged leaders to use one simple sentence to express their fundamental goal or to project forward the legacy they would like to leave. Luce encouraged leaders to continually search within themselves to answer the question, "What's your *sentence*?" By phrasing her advice to focus on simplifying your personal goal into one simple sentence, Luce was simultaneously recommending that you simplify your life and refocus on what is really important—your personal truths.

Understanding our personal truths, *really* understanding them, is essential because they are the expression of our true selves. When we understand our personal truths, we liberate our fundamental energy and give ourselves the opportunity to amplify it. This amplified energy gives us increased power.

Here's the key: When leaders define, clarify, and act in lockstep with their own personal truths, the vibrating energy inside them is enhanced, and the *potential* for resonance is present.

THE FOUR OBLIGATIONS

So how do you go about defining your personal truths? And how will you know that your definition is accurate? Reflection is the gateway to personal understanding. It's also the route to personal and professional fulfillment if we are to ever simplify our lives, slow down, and become more effective.

The key lies in understanding what I call the Four Obligations:

Obligation #1. Understanding what you would die for

Obligation #2. Clarifying through doubting

Obligation #3. Committing yourself once and for all

Obligation #4. Behaving in alignment with your personal truths

We use the word *obligation* to describe each critical step in the process of defining your personal truths because an obligation is a "requirement to take some course of action." The process will give you critical insight into your personal truths. The process is iterative, and each obligation builds on the previous one (see Figure 2.1).

Our experience coaching the highest-level executive leaders in Fortune 1000 companies reveals the following: No matter what your current level of success, you will not fulfill your highest level of potential as a leader unless you adhere to these four obligations. With that in mind, let's consider each of the Four Obligations.

FIGURE 2.1 | THE FOUR OBLIGATIONS TO IDENTIFYING *YOUR* PERSONAL TRUTHS

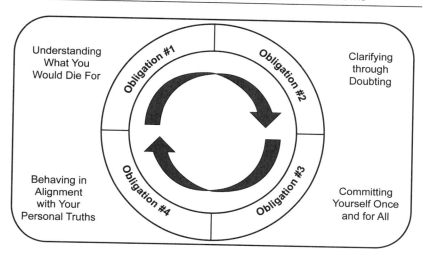

OBLIGATION #1. UNDERSTANDING WHAT YOU WOULD DIE FOR

This first obligation is where this journey begins. *You can proceed if—and only if—you complete this first step properly.* The final outcome of the process is directly affected by your effort and diligence to reflect and self-analyze.

Understanding what you would die for might sound melodramatic. No big deal here; we're simply trying to underscore the things you believe so strongly in that you would put your life in peril to protect them. It's really that important, all joking aside. Imagine the depth of your commitment when you completely understand a personal truth that is something you would die for. Even more, imagine the passion and conviction you could articulate when something is this important to you. The frequency of the vibrating energy inside you becomes palpable when you are living a life consistent with a personal truth this important to you. Watch Martin Luther King's "I Have a Dream" speech and feel the depth of his commitment to his personal truth that freedom is a universal human right; King was truly willing to die for this personal truth, and he did.

You also can flip this coin and view it from another perspective: What mission or purpose do you *live* for? What makes you forge ahead and persevere, even when your efforts are like those of Sisyphus, doomed to push an immense boulder up a hill for eternity, only to watch it roll back down repeatedly?

My dad is from Tom Brokaw's aptly named "Greatest Generation." He was born in 1921, lived through the Great Depression, and fought in World War II. As a staff sergeant in the 928th Field Artillery Battalion, medical detachment, he stormed Normandy Beach; before that he fought in the bloody Italian campaign under General Patton. One of his favorite stories, one of only a few he shared on the war, was when he was marching on a dirt road during the Italian campaign and his unit was suddenly under fire. As his unit was strafed by German planes, he jumped into the ditch on the side of the road just in time to see General Patton's jeep cruise by. Patton stood in the jeep, taunting the planes, and yelling curse words at them. At a very young age, my dad was willing to die for his commitment to this country . . . and he was led by a general who also had a very clear willingness to die for his cause.

My dad taught me the power of a strong will to overcome seemingly impossible odds. He learned to persevere under the most horrific circumstances imaginable. When I reflect on his experience and who he became as a result, I see how perseverance has become a personal truth of mine. Throughout my career, I can point out instances where my will to persevere carried me through a very difficult set of circumstances and ended in success. When you are in touch with your personal truths and behaving accordingly, you suddenly have the capacity to do what "the experts" say can't be done. The same is true for you as you attempt to lead a high-energy culture. Maybe the odds are against you, and maybe people are telling you something can't be done. But if you stay focused and believe in your vision while refusing to give in until you fulfill it, you might stun everyone, including yourself.

OBLIGATION #2. CLARIFYING THROUGH DOUBTING

Leonardo da Vinci was one of the most gifted—and disciplined— human beings in recorded history. His artistic skill is what most defines his genius. What lay behind his extraordinary skill? He had very powerful personal truths. They were:

- *Curiosità*. His insatiable curiosity

- *Sensazione*. His heightened development and use of his five senses

- *Dimostrazione*. His discipline to always test what he thought and believed

These truths distinguished him as a Renaissance man. All three qualities were manifest in his genius, but it is *dimostrazione* that is so brilliant and relevant to this process.

Da Vinci held that truth and wisdom came from experience. Furthermore, an important aspect of experience was the necessity of testing your beliefs. Da Vinci trained himself to look at a particular conclusion, whether it was the subject of a painting or sculpture, an idea, or a concept, from three separate and distinct points of view. He was essentially able to completely set aside one viewpoint, place himself in an entirely different mindset, and view the subject from the new and totally different angle. Then he was able to do this a third time. This technique would help da Vinci avoid false conclusions and ultimately confirm his belief, prompting a course of action. The number of masterpieces that he produced is a testament to the power of this process.

Similarly, you are obligated to clarify your own personal truths with the same rigor. To do so, make an argument against one of your beliefs as a second point of view. You may solicit input from your closest friend or a family member—someone who can give you insight that you may not have considered. A third perspective may involve focusing on your feelings as you deliberate on the personal truth. We'll walk through this as we do the exercises later in this chapter. The important outcome is that you want to clarify your PTs, eliminating any false PTs that you may have up until now accepted as truths. This takes time, effort, and intense observation. When done correctly, it can result in a sudden realization that is quite jolting.

A personal example hit me like a knockout punch while I was riding in the car with my son. He was a freshman in high school, and I was driving him to baseball practice. We were alone in the car, and I was seething about a poor grade on his report card, which I had just reviewed before picking him up. My son has very keen radar, and so he knew I was unhappy about something. The ride was a silent one until I chose to break the silence. I said, "I got your report card today, Andrew." Still silence. I continued, trying to balance the anger and disappointment with anything positive I could muster: "I am happy that your teacher's comments are positive . . .," then the inevitable "*but* what happened in math?"

My anger had overtaken me at that point, and so I don't recall what Andrew said to me, but I do recall that I said very frankly, "The problem is one of two things, Andrew. Either you aren't as smart as I thought, or you simply aren't working hard enough. I know you're smart, so it can *only* be the latter." The end of this statement was much louder than the beginning. Staring straight ahead with his chin up, my son sat there as tears welled up in his eyes. I recall seeing him conjure up all the courage he had inside with a quiet sniffle and a short breath or two. Then he said, "Dad, I don't get it. I *am* working hard. I'm sorry to disappoint you, but I am not as smart as you thought." My son is not one to give excuses. His response shut me down.

During a long conversation with one of his teachers, I eventually learned that Andrew really was telling the truth that day. I was good at math. I assumed my son was too. And in making this assumption I neglected his need for support.

I've reflected on this moment many times since that day. By looking at this from multiple angles, through conversations with my wife, and through reflection on my own experience as a son, a personal truth was removed from my list on that day, and it was replaced by another. It effectively recentered my thinking regarding a personal truth related to our children. Love them, listen to them, encourage them . . . but don't see them as you.

Probably the two greatest failures of leaders are indecisiveness in times of urgent need for action and dead certainty that they are right in times of complexity.

—MICHAEL FULLAN, EDUCATOR
AND LEADERSHIP AUTHOR

As a business leader, you are guided by your personal truths when making decisions, particularly in difficult times or periods of crisis. Clarifying your PTs now will avert misguided decisions and actions in the future. Your business and those you lead depend on you and the authenticity of your truths.

OBLIGATION #3. COMMITTING YOURSELF ONCE AND FOR ALL

Personal truths are actionable. They aren't just "nice ideas." A primary reason we define a PT as "one you would die for" is to ensure that you commit yourself to acting on it. Committing yourself to your newfound personal truths is the next step and the subject of Chapter 3. Suffice to say here that the act of *committing* is not as easy as the word may imply.

A great example is Mahatma Gandhi and the concept of *satyagraha*, a Sanskrit word roughly translating to "soul force." However, breaking down the word better shows its connection to this chapter:

▸ *Satya* = truth

▸ *Graha* = insistence or firmly holding to

So *satyagraha* literally refers to an insistence on the truth. In Gandhi's words: "In the application of satyagraha, I discovered in the earliest stages that pursuit of truth did not admit of violence being inflicted on one's opponent but that he must be weaned from error by patience and compassion. For what appears to be truth to the one may appear to be error to the other. And patience means self-suffering. So the doctrine came to mean vindication of truth, not by infliction of suffering on the opponent, but on oneself."

This principle is fundamental to his concept of active resistance. It also resulted in one of the most memorable moments in the film *Gandhi*, where hordes of Indians march up to British soldiers and allow themselves to be struck down without striking back. It only happened because so many of his followers were willing to commit once and for all to the personal truth that he had defined: Colonial rule by the British was wrong and needed to end.

Obligation #4. Behaving in Alignment with Your Personal Truths

As a leader, and as a human being, when you are clear on your core personal truths, you have a foundation on which to build your leadership and your legacy. Your behaviors are witness to the outside world of your defined personal truths. In a business context, this trait is sometimes referred to as "walking the talk."

Say what you want, but if you do not *do* as you say, then the world will see through your words. It's that simple. Courage and discipline are the keys to behaving in alignment with your truths. As we will explore thoroughly in Chapter 3, you are eminently more likely to be courageous and disciplined when you are clear on your PTs.

LEARN FROM THE IMPORTANT PEOPLE IN YOUR LIFE

As you go through the four-step obligation process to define your personal truths, you'll undoubtedly find yourself reflecting on the important people in your life—just as Ra'ad Siraj did when he talked about his father at the beginning of this chapter.

Throughout this book, I'll encourage you to reflect on the people who have been essential to your growth and development, as you did in the exercise you completed at the end of Chapter 1. This is a key factor in understanding your personal truths. Why? Because when you recognize which people had the greatest impact on you in terms of your values, you have the opportunity to analyze how their values affected them, and thus, more objectively understand your values. Figure 2.2 sums up the reflection process.

As you continue to navigate your path to leadership effectiveness, you will periodically reflect on these significant people and their values. When these reflections come to the forefront of your consciousness, capture them in note form or you may lose them. Their importance to you is profound, because they define your personal truths. The exercises at the end of this chapter will help you continue this process.

FIGURE 2.2 | STEPS TO PERSONAL TRUTHS

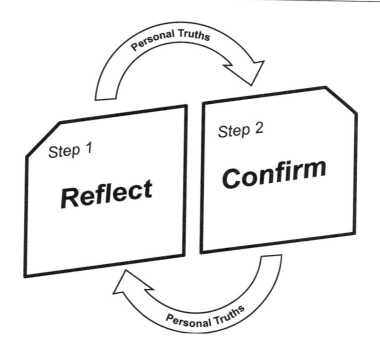

BEWARE FALSE CONCLUSIONS

This builds on the earlier idea of clarifying through doubting. When you begin the process of reflection, it is very important to consider all options and remain open to possible personal truths that *may* qualify as your own.

A word of caution: Beware of false conclusions. Sometimes we can fall prey to our egos and believe something to be true when in reality, when tested, it proves otherwise. Mel Schwartz, acclaimed psychotherapist and author, says, "When we are firmly entrenched in our beliefs, and rooted in certainty, we're not typically open to insights."

Pfeffer and Sutton preface their perspective on their observation that "in numerous industries ranging from gaming to baseball to education, failure to find and follow the best logic and evidence leads to relying on conventional wisdom that is frequently incorrect or incomplete, and as a consequence, downright hazardous to organizational health." Applying their observation to *beliefs*, they further assert that "beliefs that are total nonsense do harm and must be debunked . . . however, even greater damage is done by beliefs that are partly right and apply at certain times, but when treated as completely true and applied in full force to every decision and every action, undermine performance, destroy management careers, and ruin employee well-being."

Pfeffer and Sutton assert that "traveling through life with an attitude of wisdom—the ability to act with knowledge while doubting what you know—is the single most important quality that a leader, adviser, or team can have." What definition of wisdom could be more poignant and meaningful and of greater utility to leaders?

Michael Fullan, author, professor emeritus at the University of Toronto, and leading authority on educational change, recommends: "The message, then, is don't believe everything you read, including books on management . . . Look for the argument and the evidence behind the claims. Go deep in trying to understand the meaning . . . Develop your own theory of action by constantly testing it against situations and ideas." Thus, because beliefs are fundamental to the manner in which we make decisions and conduct ourselves, it is vital that we clarify them for our own personal understanding of them. This seems intuitive, but it's not.

So don't be romanced by the good feeling the words may create inside you. Personal truths are only feelings in part; they are more importantly actionable precepts. Remember, your most fundamental personal truths are the ones you would die for.

AN AUDIENCE OF NONE

Try this:

Imagine you are listening to yourself describe your personal truths to an audience of none—just to yourself. Do you sound genuine? Does it feel authentic? Are you moved to action?

Communicating your personal truths is a valuable litmus test, and one we will return to frequently throughout this process. Your ability to clearly communicate your PTs is imperative to creating a culture of high energy as a leader, but it is also imperative that you are able to communicate your PTs to yourself and *feel* their impact on you. Rehearsing the articulation of your PTs helps to verify their authenticity. Only you know how they feel to you. Once they are identified and understood, your PTs will energize you, they will center you, they will empower you, and they will marshal you to action. If this is not the case, keep "sifting for gold."

WHO ARE YOU?

Step 1 of this exercise challenges you to reflect on your past from two equally important perspectives—introspection and external influences. Step 2 of this exercise challenges you to reconsider your conclusions from Step 1 and either confirm or reject them. *It is important that you do not move forward until you have thoroughly and thoughtfully completed this exercise.* You may wish to take time between each step and remove yourself from the exercise. Then return and review what you have written. The accuracy of what you learn about yourself here will be challenged both in the next chapter and, more important, in real life. In the next chapter you will commit to and act on what you learn here.

STEP 1. REFLECTION

Suppose I asked you the simple question, "Who are you?" What would you say? Stop for a moment and really think about this. *Who are you?*

In three sentences or less, write your answer to the question "Who am I?"

_____

_____

_____

_____

_____

If you found this simple exercise easy, good for you! You are in the minority. Regardless, it's important to stay with the process because what you will learn may surprise you. If you found this simple exercise more difficult than you anticipated, then you are like most people who are confronted with this simple, straightforward question. You likely found yourself starting and stopping thoughts, then shifting direction. Perhaps the broad scope of the simple question may have had you thinking in multiple contexts. Who am I personally? Or who am I professionally? Your thought may have been, "Well, I am a parent." Or "I am a leader." If you have a cynical bent, you may have simply said, "I am a human being." It's all good. Stay with me here.

Now let's narrow the scope of the question and take a second introspective look at ourselves. Think about how you might answer this question, "Who am I when I'm with my closest friend?" Stop reading and think about this.

In three sentences or less, write your answer to the question, "Who am I when I am with my closest friend?"

_____

_____

_____

_____

_____

Perhaps this answer differs in some way from your answer to the first question. If so, how does it differ? If it does not, then move on.

_____

_____

_____

_____

Now let's reflect on a time when one of your key truths was shattered—a paradigm buster. It might have happened in college, in an early job experience, or through some friendship or relationship. Regardless, it should be an event or experience that permanently changed a personal truth.

What experience in your past was a paradigm buster for you?

_____

_____

_____

_____

_____

_____

_____

_____

_____

Next, recall a personal traumatic experience—a life-threatening illness, the death of a family member or friend. This may be difficult at first. You may find that you have blocked out much of the experience because it was enormously upsetting. That's understandable. However, often these traumatic experiences are also opportunities. These reveal fundamental truths that above everything else are most important to you. Try to recall what came to mind in the midst of the trauma. What was important? What became incidental that you typically hold up as important? Capture what you learned from the story by writing it here.

_____

_____

_____

_____

_____

Finally, let's reflect on something Kouzes and Posner call "your personal best leadership experience." Think of a time in your career when you were leading a team, a department, or an organization when you were at your very best. Athletes refer to this type of experience as "being in the zone." Try to mentally place yourself back into that moment. What was the situation? Describe it thoroughly. What prompted you to act? How did you feel as you were leading the group through this situation? It is important to capture the stimuli and your response to each. Use a separate sheet of paper.

STEP 2. CONFIRMATION—THE ACID TEST

Warning to the wise, "Act with knowledge while doubting what you know."

—PFEFFER AND SUTTON, LEADERSHIP
RESEARCHERS AND AUTHORS

The goal of this exercise will be to *doubt* everything you've written in Step 1. I call it the "acid test." We'll look at your answers from two other perspectives and either confirm or reject them. It is time to employ the genius of Leonardo da Vinci's principle *dimostrazione*—his discipline to always test what he thought and believed.

At the end of the previous chapter, you "sifted for gold." As you did so, you probably found some personal truths that *seem* to be the real thing. However, some of these may prove to be fool's gold upon closer scrutiny. Just as with real gold, we have to subject your precious nuggets to an acid test to find out which has the greatest value. What is your 24-carat personal truth?

It's not always easy to tell. We all have paradigms that we believe in. They're very powerful: They lead us to draw conclusions, sometimes based on limited evidence.

Da Vinci's concept of *dimostrazione* is all about opening your mind up to the possibility that you might be wrong. We need to open our minds and hearts to the possibility of being surprised and amazed by what we *thought* we knew . . . and by what we don't know yet. It's admirable—and scary—to challenge what we may have believed for a long time. But this process can lead you to capture your most defining personal truth.

Leaders have got to stand for something. You have to get off the fence and make a statement about who you are. A genuine, authentic personal truth is the core of your vision, words, and actions, and it's an irresistible force that will attract customers, investors, and employees. People will absolutely believe you when they know that you're speaking from the core of your very soul.

So now let's subject your tentative personal truths to an acid test to help you separate the true gold from the pyrite.

For each of your top four personal truths, rank your level of agreement with each statement on the worksheets. Then give yourself points for each answer as shown on the worksheets: from +2 for "strongly agree" to −2 for "strongly disagree." Add up your total and see which of the four personal truths yielded the most points when subjected to your acid test.

Personal Truth #1: _____

Point Total: _____

Statement	Strongly Disagree (–2)	Disagree (–1)	Neutral (0)	Agree (+1)	Strongly Agree (+2)
I would not accept a job making $1 million per year if this truth would not be fulfilled or honored.					
This must be a regular part of my professional life to make me excited to go to work each day.					
When I talk to friends and family outside of work, this theme often comes up in the stories and lessons that I'm eager to share.					
When I've felt frustrated or unfulfilled in the past, it's because this element has been lacking.					
My spouse, partner, or closest friend would be quick to mention this as one of my defining traits.					
When I have the opportunity to do work that relates to this value, I am absolutely "in the moment" and energized.					

Personal Truth #2: _____

Point Total: _____

Statement	Strongly Disagree (–2)	Disagree (–1)	Neutral (0)	Agree (+1)	Strongly Agree (+2)
I would not accept a job making $1 million per year if this truth would not be fulfilled or honored.					
This must be a regular part of my professional life to make me excited to go to work each day.					
When I talk to friends and family outside of work, this theme often comes up in the stories and lessons that I'm eager to share.					
When I've felt frustrated or unfulfilled in the past, it's because this element has been lacking.					
My spouse, partner, or closest friend would be quick to mention this as one of my defining traits.					
When I have the opportunity to do work that relates to this value, I am absolutely "in the moment" and energized.					

Personal Truth #3: _____

Point Total: _____

Statement	Strongly Disagree (–2)	Disagree (–1)	Neutral (0)	Agree (+1)	Strongly Agree (+2)
I would not accept a job making $1 million per year if this truth would not be fulfilled or honored.					
This must be a regular part of my professional life to make me excited to go to work each day.					
When I talk to friends and family outside of work, this theme often comes up in the stories and lessons that I'm eager to share.					
When I've felt frustrated or unfulfilled in the past, it's because this element has been lacking.					
My spouse, partner, or closest friend would be quick to mention this as one of my defining traits.					
When I have the opportunity to do work that relates to this value, I am absolutely "in the moment" and energized.					

Personal Truth #4: _____

Point Total: _____

Statement	Strongly Disagree (–2)	Disagree (–1)	Neutral (0)	Agree (+1)	Strongly Agree (+2)
I would not accept a job making $1 million per year if this truth would not be fulfilled or honored.					
This must be a regular part of my professional life to make me excited to go to work each day.					
When I talk to friends and family outside of work, this theme often comes up in the stories and lessons that I'm eager to share.					
When I've felt frustrated or unfulfilled in the past, it's because this element has been lacking.					
My spouse, partner, or closest friend would be quick to mention this as one of my defining traits.					
When I have the opportunity to do work that relates to this value, I am absolutely "in the moment" and energized.					

CHAPTER 3

Remove the Shroud

> *Courage: the most important of all virtues because without courage, you can't practice any other virtue consistently.*
> —MAYA ANGELOU, AMERICAN AUTHOR AND POET

In the opening episode of *The Paper Chase*, a 1978–1979 television series about first-year Harvard Law student James Hart, our protagonist arrives late to his first class with legendary professor Charles W. Kingsfield, Jr. Even worse, he has not read the assigned material.

When this becomes evident, Professor Kingsfield—played by legendary actor John Houseman—walks over and throws an imaginary funeral shroud over the law student. Basically, he has pronounced that the student is dead to him now. Why should the professor waste his valuable time on someone who is clearly not ready to put in the necessary effort—the price of admission to the classroom dialogue?

Hart is in a panic. He tries to talk to his venerable professor afterward but is rebuffed. He arrives ultra prepared for the next few classes . . . and he is positively ignored. How will he recover from being "shrouded"?

Finally, he comes up with an answer. He arrives at class wearing an actual funeral shroud. As he sits motionless in his chair, the class is abuzz to see what will happen. The professor is startled, but he finally asks a question of young James Hart . . . who ignores him! Professor Kingsfield asks louder and finally shouts. Nothing doing . . . until he walks over and yanks the shroud off the student. At this point, Hart bursts into the definitive answer to the question. The professor drops the shroud on the floor while listening carefully, ready to engage in dialogue. Now the shroud has been lifted figuratively as well as literally.

The student had arrived at Harvard Law School believing he was committed to doing what was necessary to become the best lawyer he was capable of becoming, but he initially failed to take action on that noble idea. His professor challenged his commitment, revealing the student's lack of courage to truly commit, and so the funeral shroud became the metaphor to describe the impediment to true commitment.

Now that the shroud had been removed, he would not fail to act on his commitment to becoming an outstanding lawyer.

A FOCUS ON ACTION

In this chapter, we will talk about honoring your personal truths and embracing them as a call to action. A key theme of this book, as you have likely begun to notice, is the focus on *action*. As a practitioner, I learned by observing others *behaving* in alignment with these concepts and by experiencing them myself through action. The great leaders I have learned from and those I participate with today are "doers." They wait for no one. In fact, they tend to grow impatient quickly. They know what is important, lower their heads, and press forward, modeling Nike's "Just Do It" motto.

In Chapter 2, we introduced the concept of the Four Obligations. We focused on the first and second obligations—understanding and clarifying your personal truths—which are "actionable." Now, we'll turn to the third obligation, commitment to action. The fact that you've identified and clarified *actionable* personal truths is important and perhaps the primary distinction between the commonly accepted definitions of *values* and our *personal truths*. PTs, indeed, are actionable. In fact, if you don't act on them, they lose their value, and the amplifying effect on your inner vibrations is lost. Many organizations have crafted lofty vision statements that are entirely actionable. But what happened? The vision statement was framed and hung up in the lobby . . . where it now has no meaning or relevance whatsoever.

Worse yet, once PTs are clear, lack of action can dampen existing vibrations and actually de-energize you . . . or even worse, turn the energy back into a loose live wire that delivers an unpleasant jolt. This happens because you are now all too aware of your personal truths. They are no longer nebulous. They have moved from the subconscious to the conscious, amplifying your resonant energy in the process. If you choose *not* to act on them, your awareness of this betrayal is psychologically demotivating and ultimately reverses the amplification process. If, over an extended period of time, you lack the courage to act on your personal truths, the energy within is likely to be reduced to a level *below* the point it was *before* you started this process. Alternatively, the energy remains but becomes a negative force, and the individual plugs into unproductive political behavior.

You must commit to action. Acting positively on your personal truths is the key to getting your energy to the point where it can resonate throughout your organization.

This chapter is about having the courage to act on the personal truths you have identified, clarified, and confirmed, fueling the energy you need to move forward (see Figure 3.1). It is about unveiling the "new you"—coming out from behind the curtain, glowing with the energy from your new self-understanding. It is about overcoming any obstacle to action and forsaking any previously embedded impediment that is preventing you from acting on the courage of your convictions. Sometimes having courage requires a catalyst.

GEOFF'S GIFT

For me, Geoff Davis provided such a catalyst. Geoff was a friend, a neighbor, and one of the most respected school administrators in New York State. In many ways he was a latter-day da Vinci. He was a Renaissance man—he had a Ph.D. in education, was a "go-to" authority for public administrators in New York State for education, played drums in a rock band, loved Audi automobiles, and was one of the finest gentlemen I have ever known. He adored his children and his wife, Cindy. Geoff

FIGURE 3.1 | THE ENERGY CONTINUUM

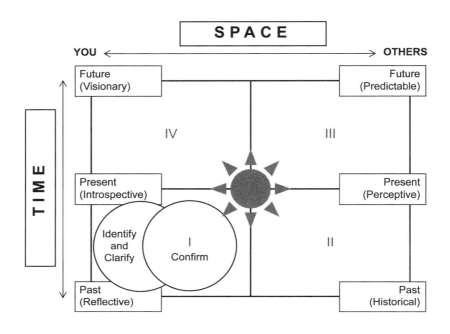

was blessed with a keen intellect, but it was his ethic and his disciplined diligence that set him apart from others who were similarly blessed.

Geoff was as much a student of leadership as he was a leader himself, which became the common denominator that drew us closer over time. He and I regularly talked about leadership and were delighted to learn that we shared similar philosophies on the subject. Both of us had a deep desire to pursue a career in leadership development beyond our prosaic lives. Because of our respective experiences, both of us felt there was a substantial demand for what we had learned. More important, we both wanted to leave a legacy. Our leadership skills and knowledge seemed to give us the best opportunity. Most important, we thought it could make a difference. We were driven to make a difference, and we were up for the challenge.

In early 2009, we began seriously discussing the possibility of collaborating on a unique leadership development concept when, out of the blue, Geoff was diagnosed with cancer. It was just after his oldest son's wedding. The consummate "type A" personality, Geoff was always moving at top speed. He was built for it. He was athletic and trim, did not smoke, and drank only occasionally. So although the diagnosis was not good—malignant melanoma—this didn't stop Geoff. As with any difficult challenge he had faced in his career, this one would be met head-on and with no thought of failure. Geoff denied his disease was terminal right up until the moment he passed away.

I remember that morning. As I looked out my living room window to the valley below, I could see Geoff and Cindy's house. The lights of the ambulance in his driveway were flashing, but there was an eerie lack of urgency in the people standing out in front of Geoff's house. I knew what I did not want to admit to myself.

I wish this were a story that ended with Geoff's courage saving his life, but Geoff passed at the unfairly young age of 53. Although he never allowed himself to believe it would happen, some aspects of our destiny cannot be changed with sheer determination, even if you're Geoff Davis.

His death shook me to my core. In fact, I'm still shaken. His absence robbed me and all those who could have benefited from his wisdom, his experience, and his example going forward. It was Geoff's passing that clarified for me, once and for all, who I am and what I need to do. Perhaps it was Geoff's gift to me.

CATALYSTS OF ACTION

Geoff's courage as he was dying was as inspiring as his actions during a robust life. As an extraordinary leader in education, alive with his passion and a resonant energy to make a difference, he lifted everyone around him and energized the regional school systems he led. As an exemplary school administrator Geoff was awarded posthumously New York State's highest honor, the New York State Council of Superintendent's Lifetime Distinguished Service Award. The executive director of the council said, "In this day of standards, Geoff was and remains *the* standard of excellence for [superintendents]." Geoff's example of leadership and courage prompted me to act. While one can be prompted to act by the inspiring example of a friend, there are other powerful catalysts of action, such as *duty* and *unrest*.

*Let us have faith that right makes might, and in that faith, let us,
to the end, dare to do our duty as we understand it.*

—ABRAHAM LINCOLN, SIXTEENTH
PRESIDENT OF THE UNITED STATES

DUTY

Duty is a powerful catalyst. Rosa Parks was tired of giving in. When she refused to give up her seat on the bus to a white man that December day in 1955, she drew strength from the memories of her mother and grandmother and their courage, which she witnessed growing up. And her own act of courage now stands as a symbol to the countless others who drew strength from her leadership that day, on that bus, when duty called her name. Legendary schoolteacher Jaime Escalante once earned a comfortable living as an engineer in California. However, this failed to satisfy his sense of duty and purpose. In 1974, he quit his job in favor of teaching at Garfield High School in East Los Angeles. Initially he was so appalled at how ill prepared his students were that he asked his old employer for his job back. After some waffling, though, he decided to take on the challenge.

Ultimately, he took kids who struggled in remedial math and worked with them tirelessly until they passed the AP Calculus class. He transformed his classroom with his energy and made his supposedly unteachable students buy in to the idea that they could go to college and become successful . . . if they only could master his challenging calculus class. What reaction did he get? Incredibly, an assistant principal threatened him with dismissal because he was coming to school too early, staying too late, and failing to get administrative permission before raising funds to pay for the AP tests!

When he received national attention—due largely to his story being turned into a Hollywood film called *Stand and Deliver*—he often was asked about how he did it. "The key to my success with youngsters is a very simple and time-honored tradition: hard work for teacher and student alike." He spread his high-energy culture to other teachers, and the number of students taking AP exams at Garfield jumped from 5 in 1978 to 570 in 1991, after he courageously began teaching AP Calculus to the troubled students in this same school known mainly for violence and drugs 13 years earlier.

When duty calls, it is time to act. Duty is a strong sense of responsibility to share with the world the blessing that is yours. Search your soul. What undertaking is your responsibility, your duty?

UNREST

Unrest is another powerful catalyst for action. Historically, great leaders with exemplary resonating energy like Nelson Mandela, Eleanor Roosevelt, and Martin Luther King, Jr., were motivated in part by *unrest*. Mandela spent decades in jail for fighting apartheid before finally emerging victorious as the president of South Africa; Eleanor Roosevelt was spurred to action by the unrest of working women in the United States and the persistent urge to promote basic human rights around the world; and Martin Luther King was inspired by the unrest of an entire race of people deprived of the freedom that is their inalienable right. These leaders, as so many others throughout history, were prompted to act by unrest. What is left undone that you have the power to change?

Duty and unrest are catalysts for action, and they become remarkable when they expose your commitment to your personal truths. Where they are clear and present, there is a strong desire to act that is inextricably linked to the burning in the leader's belly. This link between duty and unrest and the burning desire inside drives an extraordinary commitment to act. This deep level of commitment points to a primary cause of *self-motivation*, which is a fundamental attribute of successful leaders.

Let's take a closer look at commitment.

THE SECRET TO COMMITMENT

Kouzes and Posner's research in their seminal work, *The Leadership Challenge*, profoundly correlates commitment to clarity of personal values. Their work states that people who are clear on what is important to them are more committed to their organizations than other members. This commitment is strongest when the organization's values are clear and the members of the organization are clear on their own personal values. Where there is a positive correlation between personal and organizational values, members have a heightened level of commitment to the organization's success.

This concept fascinated me during my days with furniture retailer Raymour & Flanigan, where I was charged with creating a Leadership Development Institute. Clarity of values, which we defined as "enduring beliefs," was a fundamental imperative to commitment. The more we studied this concept, the more apparent it became that self-motivation, like commitment, was correlated with clarity of values as well. We consistently found that when our highest-potential leaders suddenly became crystal clear on their values, they were motivated to perform at a higher level, just as Kouzes and Posner's research had demonstrated.

Never ones to simply accept the principle, we had to ask ourselves why. Then we noticed something more profound and compelling. Of the nearly 500 potential leaders who had participated in the intensive development process, only 18 percent of the participants showed increased performance, postdevelopment. These were the people who had earned roles of increased responsibility through promotions and demonstrated a definitively higher level of leadership effectiveness in key areas such as business strategy, development of other leaders, performance against measured targets, and commitment to the company and its strategic direction.

Just as interesting, 68 percent of the participants seemed to grasp the concepts and left the formal education portion of the program motivated to apply what they learned. They articulated a desire to continue to develop these concepts, but they showed no demonstrable improvement in their leadership effectiveness over time. Eventually, they appeared to lose any motivation that was gained from their participation in the classroom portion of the institute.

The bottom 14 percent either moved out of the organization or simply failed. There is a noteworthy distinction here. Not all of the people in this bottom group who chose to stay with the company and either were demoted to lower levels of responsibility or were terminated were viewed as "failures." Some members of this group, through their intense introspection, clarified personal truths that were out of alignment with the organization. Equipped with far greater self-awareness regarding their

FIGURE 3.2 | CLARITY OF PERSONAL VALUES

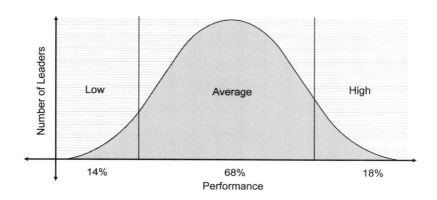

personal truths, they left the company with renewed focus and clarity, often flourishing when they landed with an organization that resonated with their own needs. They often thanked us for helping them "find their way," and the organizations they migrated to were influenced positively by their energy. Others in this bottom group, however, either did not buy in to the process, and thus were not committed to doing the hard work of introspection, or were engaged in a discovery process that was flawed in some way, meaning the conclusions they made regarding their PTs were ultimately incorrect. Overall, and somewhat predictably, the results of our development effort followed the statistical normal curve (see Figure 3.2).

We became determined to identify the differentiating characteristic(s) of the 18 percent in the top group. It seemed that this could be the secret to developing successful leaders organically that would give our company an enormous competitive advantage. What we found is the essence of this book.

THE FIVE C'S

Our first inclination was to define the differentiating qualities that were common to the leaders in the top group. We called these common differentiators the *five C's* (see Figure 3.3). Let's take them one by one.

FIGURE 3.3 | THE FIVE C'S

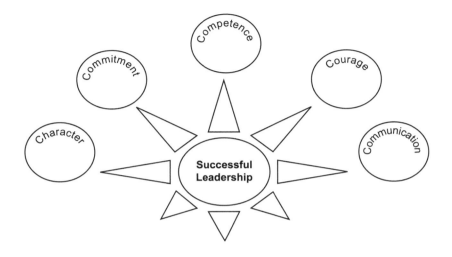

CHARACTER

Much has been written about *character* as it relates to leadership. Today, character and integrity are generally accepted as the price of entry to top leadership roles, particularly on the heels of the tumultuous ethical breaches that led to the Sarbanes-Oxley Act. Whether you are a CEO of a large public company or a member of the executive leadership team, sound character is a requirement or your company is at risk. In reality, the importance of sound character extends to everyone in a leadership role, whether she is bound to the terms of federal law or not. Nothing has as big an impact on those who choose to follow the leader more than character, or a lack thereof.

In business, as in life, character is determined by a leader's actions more than by her words. When you are "in the seat," people are watching what you do. They scrutinize how you behave and consciously or subconsciously compare how you behave with what you say.

This came as a particularly sobering realization for my wife and me in the realm of parenting, perhaps the most important leadership role any of us undertakes. Interestingly, the parenting lesson emerged from the executive leadership development process. A key element of our leadership development program was the reflection exercise called "My Leadership Point of View," because it was typically the catalyst for the "aha" moment when participants realized there was something important deep inside themselves that they had forgotten. As homework between sessions, we asked the participants to write about someone in their past who had a profound impact on them and why. We were very careful not to imply that it had to be a positive effect, because we felt strongly that a negative influence could have as meaningful an impact on a person's value development as could a positive influence.

The results were eye opening. Over 70 percent of the participants wrote about a parent, which made sense intuitively. But our expectations were that other influences would come into play more frequently than they did. That was not the most compelling or surprising observation, however. What was truly amazing was that participants wrote almost equally as frequently about the *negative* influence a parent had on them as they did those who had a positive influence. Their personal truths were formed by what they witnessed in a parent—good or bad. Often it was what the parent did that so disheartened them that they committed to *never doing the same thing themselves*. They committed to a counteraction as a personal truth.

As a parent myself, I was immediately thrown into a panic of reflection, hoping to learn that my actions did not cause a similar reaction with my children. What had become so vivid to me was how parents' actions, not words, have such a powerful impact on their children. Similarly, as leaders in our respective organizations, it is our *actions* that matter most. *Character* is revealed by our actions, and most particularly in times of difficulty.

COMMITMENT

The leadership development experience also revealed a lot about the drivers of *commitment*. Most good leaders have no trouble gaining *compliance* from their subordinates: They can get people to do what they are told to do. But that's not nearly the same as inspiring commitment. Perhaps more than any other indicator of effective leadership, commitment of one's followers to the leader denotes excellence. Leaders yearn to have committed followers. Commitment to the leader, to the company, and to the business strategy is what drives business results.

Your leadership competency, it turns out, determines commitment to the company and the business strategy from those who follow you. People will find it very difficult to believe in the company or the business strategy if they cannot believe in their leader. Kouzes and Posner called this the "First Law of Leadership." Your people's commitment, therefore, is a function of your clarity about your personal truths. It's also testament to the *accuracy* of your personal truths as well as *your courage to act* on them.

The leaders in the development program who ended up in the bottom 14 percent of the normal curve, those who left the company or were asked to leave, were often committed to their personal truths when it came to saying the right words. What was enlightening—and different from the top-performing leaders—was the observation that personal truths expressed by the bottom 14 percent were often inaccurate, meaning that their words did not truly reflect the "who that the person was." Those were just words, often spoken resolutely and with passion, but just words nonetheless. The people's actions did not reflect their words.

Integrity and character are simply personal truths in action. Your actions as a leader determine the accuracy of your personal truths and the depth of your commitment and your people's commitment. Do what you say you will do!

To be an authentic leader, to behave consistently with your defined personal truths and to tap the energy within, you must understand, clarify, *and* act on your personal truths because this is what drives commitment.

DRILLING DEEPER

Why were the people in the top 18 percent group more self-motivated than the rest? This is where the team's efforts to understand really paid off. These people were noticeably more *self-motivated* to a much higher degree than the 68 percent in the "average" category. Something inside them created a level of self-motivation that went beyond the *normal* motivating effect of just clarifying their values. Clarifying their values catalyzed action inside these extraordinary leaders. It became apparent that the top 18 percent demonstrated a differentiating level of courage to act on their personal truths—this was a key impetus to the resonating energy inside them moving outward to create the potential for resonating energy within their organization. Courage was the single most important factor that gave their potential energy economic value to the firm.

What drove *courage* in the top 18 percent of our leaders?

COMPETENCE

The competence that engenders confidence and then courage (see Figure 3.4) begins with skill development. The right leaders demonstrate strong performance consistently. They bring results. In business, they are trusted because they are reliable. Trust in business is as much a function of competence as it is character. Effective leaders know what to do and how to do it. They are skilled. Billions of dollars are spent on executive development in corporations, year after year. The dedicated people in charge of these programs apply enormous energy and resources figuring out how to achieve the desired outcomes. Yet they often forget one critical factor—developable leaders *want* development. They are skilled, but *they know what they don't know*. They want to further develop their skills and learn more skills. As Kouzes and Posner postulated, leadership development at its core is continual self-development. You can't teach desire—the best leaders bring it to the table, and they bring it to the table in the form of courage. Developable leaders are confident people.

When we coach executives, we find there is enormous value to having leaders review digital videos that reveal their leadership communication styles. It gives executives a perspective they often do not truly understand otherwise. Those who are honest and open to needing

FIGURE 3.4 | SKILL DEVELOPMENT

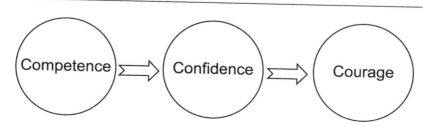

improvement act on it. They practice the skill that they need to create the behavior they wish to internalize. Practice develops skill and drives competence, and *competence* is the third C.

> *The difference between talent and skill is an insane work ethic.*
>
> —WILL SMITH, AMERICAN ACTOR,
> TELEVISION AND FILM PRODUCER,
> AND RAPPER

When it comes to the hours they devote to their sports, professional athletes are at practice 90 percent of the time and are in game situations the other 10 percent. They have the luxury of time to practice. Given this disparity, one factor that creates a distinctive competitive advantage is *how* the athlete or the team practices. Other factors include team chemistry, overall innate talent, work ethic, and preparation. But it's how the athlete or team practices that primarily determines the level of skill on game day.

Vince Lombardi, the famous pro football coach of the champion Green Bay Packers, was known for his obsessive attention to detail. His practice sessions included meticulous repetition of the relatively few plays in their playbook so players would react instinctively to the opponent's defensive strategy on game day. As Bart Starr, his Hall of Fame quarterback, reflects, Vince told his players, "We are going to relentlessly pursue perfection, knowing full well that we will not catch it. We are going to relentlessly chase it because in the process we *will* catch excellence." Lombardi went on to say, "I am not the least bit interested in just being good." The secret to competence is a commitment to practice. The secret to excellence is an "insane" commitment to practice.

For business leaders, the ratio of practice time to game time is reversed. Business leaders are in the game 90 percent of the time and have 10 percent, at best, to practice. For business leaders, skill development is a time challenge. This is why executive-level leaders are expected to have technical and business competence when they reach that level.

In his book *Outliers*, Malcolm Gladwell reflects on a large body of research in many different fields with regard to the effect that practice has on performance. He finds that "the people at the top don't just work harder or even much harder than everyone else. They work much, *much* harder. "The idea is that excellence at performing a complex task requires a critical minimum level of practice again and again in studies of expertise. In fact, researchers have settled on what they believe is the magic number for true expertise: ten thousand hours."

Gladwell quotes neurologist Daniel Levitin, who wrote, "The emerging picture from such studies is that ten thousand hours of practice is required to achieve the level of master associated with being a world-class expert—in anything. In study after study, of composers, basketball players, fiction writers, ice skaters, concert pianists, chess players, master criminals, and what have you, this number comes up again and again. Of course, this doesn't address why some people get more out of their practice sessions than others do. But no one has yet found a case in which true world-class expertise was accomplished in less time."

Competence creates confidence. The golfer on the first tee who has practiced her driving skills to a point where she has internalized the swing mechanics necessary to give her a very reliable outcome is confident. If she has put in the "10,000 hours," the swing has become instinctual—the mechanics have become internalized.

COURAGE

As just noted—and as Figure 3.4 shows—competence creates confidence, and in turn, confidence creates courage, which over time and with enormous effort becomes instinct. The best leaders are so clear on their personal truths that acting on them becomes instinct or a learned intuition. Their efforts have confirmed their accuracy. Their truths are like bedrock that provides the foundation for everything they do. Our leaders in the top 18 percent embodied this. Their personal truths were instinctual.

Leaders whose PTs have become instinctual are special. They are unabashedly sure of themselves. They are very confident. Born of their personal truths, their confidence is not arrogant. These leaders know what is important to them, and through their actions they know from experience that their PTs serve them and those around them well.

Iris Newalu, the director of the executive education program at Smith College in Northampton, Massachusetts, is a leader who exudes resonating energy. Iris says confidently that one of her personal truths is independence and independent thinking. When she reflects on this personal truth, she recalls that her parents "never held her back" and that her entrepreneurial roots gave her the curiosity and courage to think on her own. This vibrating energy inside her energizes the women business leaders who come to Smith College for their first-class executive education program. Iris personally attends the sessions and lets her instincts help guide the women who attend. Her personal truth is that independent thinking is essential if women are to continue to gain their rightful place in business. She absolutely radiates that truth.

This level of clarity of PTs has enormous benefit to a leader. One distinctive benefit is that it promotes speed of action—particularly in times of crisis.

Rudy Giuliani is a courageous leader. His sense of duty in the midst of one of the most horrible crises imaginable compelled him to act, and to act swiftly. He immediately became highly visible, appearing frequently on radio and television. When he spoke, his words and body language were genuine and were aligned with the predominant emotions—shock, sadness, anger—yet he spoke of resolve, giving hope and courage to the New York City authorities and people affected. His presence at Ground Zero, meeting there with the workers and with the victims' families, demonstrated his gratitude and compassion. From the first moments of the unimaginable disaster, Giuliani led from the front. His clarity and understanding of his personal truths allowed him to move confidently. He had the courage of his convictions. But as Mayor Giuliani demonstrated, it is also true that you must have convictions to be courageous!

The leaders in our top 18 percent group demonstrated the courage of their convictions. In our institute setting they were tested, acted confidently and swiftly based on what they believed, and did so consistently. In their workplace, their associates were energized by this confidence and the consistency of their actions.

It is important to note that the life experiences of some of the leaders in this group were comparable to the traumatic 9/11 attack Mayor Giuliani experienced.

Our top 18 percent of leaders included veterans of war, as well as those who had suffered great personal losses, overcome life-threatening illness, or endured tumultuous family circumstances. They confirmed that reflections on these events in their past clearly shaped their personal truths. By remembering, they became committed to acting on these truths.

COMMUNICATION

Communication is all too often undervalued and overlooked. Leaders can have exemplary traits in the other four C areas, but if they cannot communicate what is inside them, in a way that inspires and motivates others, then their own energy, no matter how profound, will not resonate, period.

Whether it's in speeches, meetings, one-on-one conversations, letters, e-mails, blogs, or tweets, great leaders need to be master communicators. The bad news is that many rising executives are technically proficient but are held back by their communication skills or lack of "executive presence." The good news is that strong communication skills are themselves developable. We will spend considerable time and effort helping you develop your communication skills and competence in later chapters.

WHAT'S HOLDING YOU BACK?

Let's look at factors that may prevent you from removing that shroud and acting on your personal truths. One obvious impediment is the flip side of courage—fear. At some time in our lives, all of us experience fear. Regardless of the psychology or neurobiology of fear, what matters most to us as leaders is our reaction to fear. Fear can, and often does, determine or at worst prohibit action.

We develop fears through learning and experience. As infants, we do not feel fear; we learn it as we grow through repeated unpleasant or harmful experiences. It is also true that we conquer fear through learning and experience. Repeated rides on a roller coaster can diminish and eventually extinguish an initial fear that once seemed impossible to overcome.

Many leaders are fearful of speaking before groups, true even with many of the most senior-level and successful executives we coach. Conquering this or any other fear involves the courage to come face-to-face with it first. If you fear speaking in front of groups, then you must admit it to yourself—the first step.

Once you've faced the fear head-on, you can act to conquer it. Get help, if necessary. The support and the experience of a trusted advisor are invaluable to learning the elements of skill that are necessary to create competence and thus build the confidence that will help you overcome your fear. Plan your attack. Planning and preparation are essential now that you understand what it will take to succeed.

Don't get mired in this step, however. To help you move forward, use the formula that Colin Powell, retired four-star general and former chairman of the Joint Chiefs of Staff, advises. As reported in Oren Harari's article "Behind Open Doors: Colin Powell's Seven Laws of Power," Powell uses the formula P (the probability of success) = 40 to 70. This means that you shouldn't act if you have less than a 40 percent chance of being right, but don't wait to act, either. "Once the information is in the 40 to 70 range, *go with your gut*." Finally, practice, practice, practice!

The steps to conquering your fear are the steps you are taking in this book. The secret to your success in overcoming fear as a leader is the same secret to the energy within—act on your truths and you *will* act on your fears.

For some, a leader's success is credited to luck. *Luck* can be defined as the confluence of preparation and opportunity. The preparation and work you have begun and will continue through this book will not only allow you to seize opportunity as it arises; it will actually attract opportunity. Your resonant energy has an attractive force. If you choose to act on your truths, you will begin to recognize them in others—in leaders and colleagues, in family and friends. And you will be drawn to people and organizations that share your commitment to these truths. This is the law of attraction of your energy at work. When you've tapped its power, others may just perceive you as lucky—no problem; you know better. We'll talk about this more in Chapter 8.

Now that you have a new understanding of and clarity around your personal truths, your commitment to acting on them is already heightened. But you are at the metaphorical "fork in the road." You are faced with a decision. You can choose the road that you've been on, armed now with new understanding, but beware this familiar road. It may now appear smooth and safe, with many opportunities to turn back or to pull off when the weather is poor or the road conditions are treacherous, but it is a *road to mediocrity* at best. Safe though it may be, it leads around the mountain and bypasses the path to the top, where your truths shine down on those you lead and on those who see and feel them when they are around you.

The mountain path is difficult to ascend, but with the courage of your convictions it is one you can navigate to the top. As the Spanish conquistador Cortez said to his men when they arrived in what is now Mexico to conquer the Aztec Empire, "Burn the boats!" Retreat is not an option. Remove the security of a safety net that your mind conceives but your heart and soul know does not exist.

Now move to the exercises at the end of the chapter. This will be the last time in the process that we ask you to look inward. In the next chapter we will begin to shift our focus to add a different and equally important perspective—that of your organization.

TURNING POINTS

STEP 1. IDENTIFICATION AND CLARIFICATION

> *Two roads diverged in a wood, and I—*
> *I took the one less traveled by,*
> *And that has made all the difference.*
>
> —ROBERT FROST, AMERICAN POET

Throughout our lives, we have faced decision points (where two roads diverged). At these crossroads, the consequence of a decision was momentous and had a profound long-term impact. These decision points could have occurred in your personal life or in your professional life—and within the latter, in your leadership role. The road you chose at these decision points could have either led to greater success and fulfillment or taken you on a very rocky ride, one you regret.

In the space provided, identify at least one decision point in each of these three categories of your life.

Personal life #1_____

Personal life #2_____

Professional life #1_____

Professional life #2_____

Leadership role #1_____

Leadership role #2_____

Now specify whether your decision or action was one of courage or one of fear. If it was one of courage, identify, if you can, what prompted it. If it was one of fear, identify the fear.

Personal life #1_____

Personal life #2_____

Professional life #1_____

Professional life #2_____

Leadership role #1_____

Leadership role #2_____

Next, if the decision was one of courage, note whether it was prompted by the influence or inspiration of another person, or was a response to duty, or was prompted by some level of social or organizational unrest.

Personal life #1_____

Personal life #2_____

Professional life #1_____

Professional life #2_____

Leadership role #1_____

Leadership role #2_____

STEP 2. CONFIRMATION

In Chapter 1 you reflected on your personal core beliefs, and in Chapter 2 you defined your personal truths. These earlier two exercises were important to clarifying the foundation of your decisions and actions. As you now look back on the decision points in this exercise, do you find that your choices were consistent with the personal beliefs you identified in Chapter 1 and the "who that you are" in Chapter 2? Examine each of these decision points carefully.

For those decision points that were *consistent* with your personal beliefs, were those times in which you acted with courage? For those decision points that were *inconsistent* with your personal beliefs, were they those in which you acted with fear? If you find such consistency, then you have correctly identified your personal beliefs and your personal truths. If not, then you need to retrace your steps in the exercises in Chapters 1 and 2. Before you move forward, it is important that you clarify and confirm your personal truths.

CHAPTER 4

Study the Legends and Learn the Folklore

*History is a guide to navigation in perilous times. History is
who we are and why we are the way we are.*

—David C. McCullough, American author,
historian, narrator, and lecturer

In September 2006, Boeing CEO Alan Mulally received a surprising phone call. It was from Bill Ford, great-grandson of pioneering automaker Henry Ford. "We're in really tough shape, and we'd really like your help," Ford told Mulally. "Would you consider coming to Ford?"

Sharing his story with a group of Stanford MBA students in February 2011, Mulally described his early days at the legendary facility. "So I walk into the office in the world headquarters of the Ford Motor Company on the 12th floor, and I look out the window, and here's the Rouge plant," Mulally said. "And here's where Henry Ford created the moving line. This is where Mr. Toyota of Toyota came to visit to learn to make cars and how to continuously improve the quality and productivity. Here's the entire plant: At the time, it's 100% vertically integrated—the most efficient production in the world."

Yet Mulally also discovered a stark contrast between the company's rich history and its present situation. "I check with our finance people, and they give me the great news that we are projected to lose $17 billion in 2006. You can run out of money *really fast* at $17 billion a year! I also reviewed the situation about what Ford has become, and Ford had now become a house of brands. Remember that I left Boeing to come to Ford, and Ford was Aston Martin, Jaguar, Land Rover, and Volvo, and it had a significant relationship with Mazda. And it also happened to have the Ford, Lincoln, and Mercury brands."

Mulally kept finding ways in which the company had strayed from its tradition. Ford was still a worldwide operation, but there was no synergy among its branches. They were not best in class with any vehicle. In fact, every single brand and every model was losing money. No wonder the company was hemorrhaging money!

At this point in his talk, Mulally asked the members of his MBA audience what they would've done under the circumstances. They made numerous good suggestions about design, production, marketing, strategy, financing, customer focus, the Internet, and so on. Ultimately, Mulally challenged the audience with a pivotal question: "What would you use for your *vision*? What would you have rallied everybody around? You clearly are where you are, and you're going to a different place. You've just described this compelling place. How would you describe this vision? How would you describe what your new Ford is going to be like?"

One young woman in the audience delighted the Ford CEO with her response: "Go back to your history—where you came from."

"That's exactly what we did," Mulally said. "When you walk into that same office today, the entire wall is filled up with Henry Ford's vision for the Ford Motor Company that he laid out on January 24 of 1925 in the *Saturday Evening Post*. You can Google it and find it. It's fantastic. And it says: 'Opening the highways to all mankind.' That's what Henry Ford is about. He wanted to make traveling on the highways affordable and available for all of us.

"At the time, the only people who had a car were wealthy. You couldn't afford a car. He describes in this vision how it would have to be big in scale, big in scope to get the economies of scale. There would have to be a complete family of vehicles. They'd have to be best in class in safety and efficiency. They'd have to contribute to making life more pleasant, more useful. Everybody would have to participate.

"And at the time—January 24 of 1925—he's at the top of his game. He has 56% market share worldwide. Every country in the world wants Henry to come and set up his operations. He's wildly successful by any measure. And at the end of this advertisement for his vision, it says: 'It's not about what Ford has done up through 1925. This is about the opportunity to serve all the people around the world.'

"Is that incredible? So that's what we went back to. He wasn't talking about Jaguar and Aston Martin and Land Rover. He was talking about Ford. So we went to work ... We focused on the Ford brand. We decided to have a complete family of vehicles—small, medium, and large cars, utilities, and trucks—in every region around the world. We also decided that they'd be best in class in quality, fuel efficiency, safety, really smart design; and, because of our scale and our intellectual capability, absolutely the very best value."

Rallying his organization around its legends and folklore, Mulally presided over what might be the most remarkable corporate turnaround of the young century. He tapped in to the wellspring of energy originally created by Henry Ford because he intuitively sensed that it would resonate once again with Ford employees. In a matter of months, Ford was transformed into a high-energy culture ... and the impact on the bottom line was phenomenal.

SHIFT YOUR FOCUS

With the exercises in the previous chapters, you have begun the important work of understanding and clarifying your personal truths. With clarity, your personal truths have begun to increase the resonating energy inside you. Are you beginning to feel the effects of your efforts in the form of renewed self-motivation and commitment to act on your PTs?

Now it's time to shift from introspection and an internal focus to an external focus. Specifically, see if you can apply the lesson that we just learned from Alan Mulally. Focus now on the history and folklore of your organization, and if possible, on its founders and their stories. Make an effort to understand the PTs of those who were integral to the formation and growth of your company. Travel back in time to learn the stories of the people whose personal truths, vision, and courage were instrumental to the creation of your organization. This will help you better understand the root truths that define the existing energy of your culture.

In his commencement address at Stanford University in 2005, Apple founder Steve Jobs gave a speech that was simply three beautifully articulated stories from his life. He spoke of "connecting the dots," a metaphor for looking back on his life and coming to understand how his personal truths were important to the founding of his company. He spoke of trust, of following his curiosity and intuition, and of taking chances. By way of example, he referenced his curiosity about calligraphy when he was a college dropout. Fascinated by this ancient art, he attended calligraphy classes without formally enrolling because he saw no practical application for him at the time. However, one inspired day years later, he found its application as he envisioned the first Mac computer. His application of calligraphy led to the typography that is used in all computers today.

Jobs advised the Stanford graduates to have the confidence to follow their hearts. He spoke of faith, love, and loss. His most poignant reference to loss was being fired from Apple, the company he cofounded. Although rejected, he was still in love with his work. As he reflected on the experience, he came to understand that getting fired was the best thing that ever happened to him. "Sometimes life hits you with a brick," he told the graduates that day. "Don't lose faith . . . You must find what you love. Love what you do. And, as with all matters of the heart, you'll know it when you find it. Don't settle. Don't waste time living someone else's life."

Finally he left the audience with words from the *Whole Earth Catalogue*'s final edition, "Stay hungry. Stay foolish." These words of wisdom had resonated with him since the moment he first read them. Jobs's curiosity, his courage to pioneer despite knowing he'd make mistakes and even fail, his ability to learn from the mistakes, and his knack for combining art and engineering were his personal truths . . . and they define the culture of Apple. His resonating energy from these personal truths was imprinted upon Apple when his vision as founder was borne out, and these personal truths permeate the atmosphere there today. Apple's market dominance— it toppled Google when it was named the top global brand in May 2011— demonstrates how powerful truths can drive enormous economic value.

The passing of Steve Jobs in October 2011 marks the end of an era. As a CEO, he is not only an icon, he is a legend who set the bar that every other CEO will be judged against for years to come. Will his successor, Tim

Cook, be able to infuse that high-energy culture at Apple? That remains to be seen . . . but rest assured that the stories and folklore surrounding Steve Jobs will permeate the atmosphere of Apple beyond any of our lifetimes.

In this chapter, I'll explain why studying your organization's history is critical to truly understanding the present truths and sources of energy within the organization currently. It's about *curiosità*, as Leonardo da Vinci would say, an unrelenting quest for learning.

THE SOURCE OF THE NILE

The Nile is the longest river in the world—over 4,100 miles long. Going back to the times of the Roman and Greek Empires, people marveled at its power and energy, storied to have amazing life-giving vitality. Romanced by the notion of what could possibly be the origin of such power, countless explorers attempted to discover the source of the Nile for several centuries. For some, it became an obsession.

As human beings, we're fascinated by power and energy. We want to understand where it comes from. We imagine what it would be like to harness such a force as energy. And it's no different when we strive to understand a high-energy culture in the organizational world. So at this stage of the process, let's explore upstream to see where the flowing energy originates. That way, we can understand and clarify what it is—just as you have clarified your personal truths—by identifying the person or people whose PTs were fundamental to your organization's birth. Ultimately, armed with this knowledge, you'll decide how to shape your message and your vision to help your team navigate downstream to a destination that you envision.

The goals of this part of the journey are:

▶ To search for and understand your organization's truths with greater clarity

▶ To begin to identify the elements of the fundamental energy in your culture that resonate with you and your personal truths

▶ To align your personal truths with the organization's truths to amplify the energy of both

FIGURE 4.1 | THE ENERGY CONTINUUM

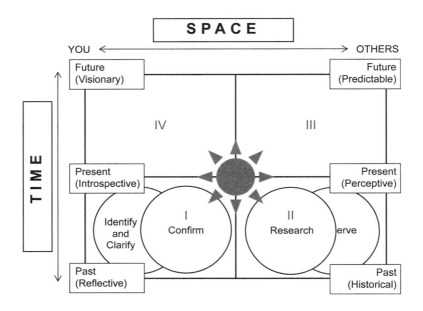

These steps are critical to leveraging the power of resonance (see Figure 4.1).

So let's start at the beginning. Your organization was formed by someone. As with Henry Ford and the Ford Motor Company or with Steve Jobs and Apple, it was conceived first as a vision in a person's mind, and that vision was shaped by this person's personal truths. The clarity of the founder's personal truths amplified the energy within him and prompted action—a defining moment. The company was born, and the concept, the Big Idea, began to take shape. Organizations have inherent energy, just as individuals do. The stream of resonating energy in your organization is already flowing, whether it has the force of the Nile or the quiet trickle of a country stream. Unless you are the founder, this energy probably came into being without your assistance.

Your organization's energy:

▸ Was formed by the personal truths of the founder

▶ Was enhanced by other leaders throughout the company's history

▶ Now exists within the atmosphere of the organization's culture

▶ Has a collective synchronizing effect on the actions of the people in your organization

For better or worse, this energy flows through your organization. It's conducted through people. Typically, this atmosphere is defined within companies—accurately or not—by their stated values, mission, and vision.

THE FOUNDER'S FINGERPRINTS

When Bob Wegman passed away in April 2006, the supermarket industry grieved the loss of one of its legendary pioneers. During his 56-year reign, Bob's leadership made Wegman's Supermarkets the benchmark for the industry. Bob was instrumental in pioneering the use of the Universal Product Code technology that is ubiquitous today. But that's only one example of how his remarkable pioneering spirit helped set his company apart. Bob's vision included the "superstore" and the "one-stop shop" concepts. By the early 1990s, a typical Wegman's store was described as a "visit to the global village." The stores were 100 times the size of the typical 1,200-square-foot stores the competition had operated for decades. Wegman's shoppers were able to purchase imported cheeses, select from restaurant-quality prepared foods, or enjoy a pastry and a latte in the store café. Wegman's was one of the first grocers to have an in-store pharmacy, a photo lab, and a video store. Shoppers with small children could comfortably let them play in the supervised child-care center while they shopped. In 1994, the *Wall Street Journal* called Wegman's "the best chain in the country, maybe in the world." Since then, Wegman's has been included in *Fortune* magazine's "100 Best Companies to Work For" list 10 times and was ranked number one in 2005.

What was the source of Bob Wegman's bountiful energy? Bob credited his father, Walter, and his Uncle Jack for teaching him the values of providing quality products, offering good customer service, and treating employees right. Bob pushed his standards to the highest levels because of the personal truths his dad and uncle instilled in him. Walter and Jack had opened their first store in 1930, combining their merchant skills in an enterprise shaped by their experience in the smallest of family businesses. Bob's dad had helped his grandmother operate a small store out of the front of their home, and his uncle had been a "huckster." Before acquiring the negative connotation it carries today, the term *huckster* at one time simply described a merchant who purchased products from the public market early in the day and then peddled the various fresh products from a cart all day long.

As you can imagine, merchandising was in Bob's blood. He was always driven to find ever-more innovative ways to satisfy the customers and make the Wegman's shopping experience memorable. His most famous speech was for a food industry conference in Thailand in 1961. It is often referred to as his "I am a merchant" speech. Even now, leaders and employees at Wegman's still refer to this speech, which has become the framework for Wegman's operating philosophy, summed up by the statement "Every Day You Get Our Best!" This remains the rallying call for the energized culture that is Wegman's today.

Bob Wegman embodied the reason Wegman's culture is unique and so successful. To understand Bob, his history, and his story is to understand Wegman's fundamental truths—the foundation on which the company is built. Today, CEO Danny Wegman, Bob's son, carries the torch that was ignited long ago inside his grandfather's and uncle's hearts. Danny's personal truths align with those of his grandfather and his uncle because his dad behaved in alignment with them. Because they resonated in his personal truths, they are now instilled in him.

The founder's influence on a company is recognized by researchers like Pfeffer and Sutton. They write: "One of the main lessons from organization theory and leadership research is that leaders exercise the greatest personal influence over a company or group when it is young, small, or both. That is why company founders have such a strong and often enduring impact on the long-term success of a company, as well as its culture, values, and way of operating." In every way a successful business flourishes, we can look and find the founder's fingerprints.

IF YOU ARE THE FOUNDER

If you are the founder of your organization, then the vibrating energy you emit permeates your organization. Your energy will determine the strength of the foundation on which your company will be built. If you are a founder, this chapter is relevant from a slightly different perspective than it will be for others.

As founder, you will become aware of how your energy flows into others and how they knowingly or unknowingly align their personal truths with yours. This awareness is enlightening and possibly humbling. You may find it humbling because you suddenly realize that the ability of others to reach their potential—today and in future generations of employees—is directly influenced by your actions. This applies not just to your direct reports but also to those who are several layers down in the organization—indeed, everyone in the organization. Just as important, the people you have hired or will hire will be profoundly affected by your personal truths. Their personal truths, their vibrating energy inside, and their highest-level motivation to be the best they can possibly be is determined, in part, by *your* behavior.

As the founder and leader, your responsibility is vastly more important than just driving business results. You are in the unique position of conceiving the company for reasons important to you. Your personal truths are uniquely fundamental to you *and* to the organization you are building. You have the ability to create something very special and meaningful in the world, and for future generations.

Founders—The organization that you've created is an extension of you. How have your personal truths manifested themselves in the formation of your organization?

THE VALUE OF LEADER ALIGNMENT

Leaders must absolutely deliver results. Sometimes they can be successful in doing so without aligning the frequency of their energy with those of the other talented people around them in the organization. However, when the frequencies are indeed misaligned, the positive results tend to be short term. And there is an often unrecognized opportunity cost associated because the results fall far below the level that can be achieved when everyone's energy is in sync.

Take, for example, Robert Nardelli, a protégé of Jack Welch at General Electric (GE) and a finalist to succeed him as the CEO. Shortly after the CEO role was awarded to Jeffrey Immelt, Nardelli was named the CEO of Home Depot. In his first five years at Home Depot, Nardelli's financial results were quite extraordinary. He doubled sales revenue and more than doubled earnings. Nardelli was out to prove that his lack of retail experience, pugnacious style of leadership, and reputation that he was "not very strategic" were all irrelevant factors. Ironically, when questioned in March 2001 by *Fortune* magazine about GE executives who were unsuccessful outside of GE as CEOs, Nardelli said that those executives "didn't realize they were in a different environment. They did not have the respect of the culture and weren't sensitive to the pride of the employees."

In saying that, he could've been looking at himself in a crystal ball. The founders of Home Depot, Bernie Marcus and Arthur Blank, had built the company on a strong platform of social responsibility. They believed the key to success was taking care of customers and associates, and they spent their time working side by side with people at every level of the organization. Blank learned this truth as a young man, thrust into helping his mother run the family wholesale pharmacy business after his father died. He and Bernie Marcus met and became close friends at Handy Dan Hardware, where a philosophical dispute with management prompted them to leave and start Home Depot. Putting people first was their mantra, and when they acted on this truth, they grew Home Depot into a retail giant.

Unlike the founders, and despite paying lip service to the idea of respecting the culture, Nardelli put performance metrics, not people, first. Although his operating principles drove efficiency and savings into the model, he neglected to align himself with the existing energy of Home Depot's culture. Ultimately, this dissonance hurt customer service, employee relations, and stock value. While the competition flourished, Home Depot suffered. In 2007, Nardelli was removed as CEO when the board of directors responded to concerns around customer service complaints, poor employee relations, and Nardelli's countercultural actions, including his exorbitant, low-risk compensation package and his cavalier treatment of shareholders at an annual meeting in late 2006.

Leaders can deliver results and yet not maximize the potential of their teams. As you work to develop yourself as a leader, you may make false assumptions that lead to incorrect conclusions. That takes you off course. At this point in the process, it is important to acknowledge the possibility of this happening and to act to mitigate the risk. As a leader, you may be good . . . but what prevents you from being great?

One common problem is with the "superstitious dance." Decades ago, psychologist B. F. Skinner experimented with hungry pigeons. He put them in a cage with a food dispenser. The pigeons would peck at the food dispenser, and nothing would happen. The food pellets were dropped at random intervals. So what happened? Eventually a pigeon might wander to a far corner of the cage, and then food would appear. The pigeon would rush over to eat the pellet . . . and then race back to the far corner of the cage! No pellet would appear immediately, but then another might pop out just as the pigeon happened to be standing on one leg. So then the pigeon would race over and eat the pellet . . . then return to the far corner of the cage and stand on one leg!

Skinner called this behavior the *superstitious dance*, and like the pigeons, we are somewhat prone to this phenomenon. When we behave a specific way and get a positive outcome, we often try to repeat the same behaviors. But what if those earlier behaviors really had nothing to do with your success? Perhaps those behaviors were *correlated* with an outcome but did not *cause* the outcome. Or what if you took actions that worked well in one setting—as they had for Nardelli—but might backfire in another situation?

Another common fallacy is the belief that the path to great leadership follows some predetermined, empirical formula. This belief may help sell leadership books, but there is no secret recipe that will work in every situation. You don't need to follow a popular recipe—or any recipe, for that matter. In fact, it may be that if you ascribe to a commonly accepted success formula, you won't succeed, because the formula conflicts with one of your abiding personal truths and thus will lead to misaligned behavior. Leaders often unintentionally embrace a methodology that actually prohibits them from becoming better because the methodology is so compelling that it actually blinds them from truly understanding *their own personal truths*.

In all walks of life, leaders sometimes make these unfounded assumptions that lead to false conclusions. Unfounded assumptions are the result of unchallenged paradigms. Paradigms are powerful influencers, sometimes powerfully good and sometimes powerfully bad influencers.

Returning to the Nardelli example again, it's clear that his experience as a GE leader afforded him the opportunity to witness firsthand the benchmark executive leadership development program in business, now called the John F. Welch Leadership Development Center at Crotonville, New York. Nardelli brought the same concepts to a similar leadership development institute at Home Depot and again ironically said the right thing but acted inconsistently with his words: "To move from one social architecture and operating system and assume it's 100% portable and the platform of understanding is there at the new place—that's a terrible mistake." It is important to challenge your beliefs and confirm the authenticity of your personal truths. As a leader, your source of strength in difficult times, and your ability to marshal action and align your troops, will be determined by the strength of the energy inside you.

If you are not the founder of your organization, it's important but not always critical to seek to understand the original founder's personal truths. What is important to you as a leader is that you understand the genesis and evolution of the organizational truths, how they have reached their current state. As with your own personal truths, you must identify and clarify your organization's truths. Understanding how they came into existence is as important as understanding the truths themselves, because otherwise your assumptions can lead to false conclusions. As we've seen, this can have dangerous consequences.

Pfeffer and Sutton provide another excellent example of the perils of a leadership decision based on a misguided assumption. They explain that in 1994 United Airlines decided to imitate the practices of Southwest Airlines in the highly lucrative intra-California marketplace. "United put its gate staff and flight attendants in casual clothes; it flew only Boeing 737s; it gave the service a different name, 'Shuttle by United,' and used separate planes and crews; it stopped serving food;

it increased the frequency of its flights and reduced the scheduled time planes spent on the ground, copying Southwest's legendary quick turn-arounds." Yet the decision was ill-fated, with Southwest actually *increasing* its market share over pre-United competition. The Shuttle initiative was a complete failure.

Why? Pfeffer and Sutton go on to say, "Southwest's success is based on its culture and management philosophy, the priority it places on its employees . . . not on how it dresses its gate agents and flight attendants, which plane it flies, or how it schedules them." Clearly, United made the assumption that practices were at the heart of Southwest's success, rather than its underlying core values. United was marveling at the river without looking for its source. And the result was a false conclusion.

LISTEN TO THE FOLKLORE

So how do you begin to find this information? A logical first step is to ask the people with longevity in the organization. Listen to the folklore, the legendary stories. These typically provide clues to the current organizational truths. Listen carefully to the stories, because they are important sources of information and good starting points for historical research.

After previous successful superintendent terms in two other public school districts, Phil Martin became superintendent of the Fayetteville-Manlius School District in the suburbs of Syracuse, New York, in 1977. What he found—and how it resonated with his personal truths—kept him there for the next 28 years. Founded in 1952, the district had a long history of educational excellence and leadership stability; only three previous superintendents had presided over its 25-year existence. What Phil found was a culture with a clear set of organizational truths: professionalism, respect for all members of the system, high expectations, continuous improvement, caring, and compassion. While Phil had been successful in his previous teaching and administrative roles, he realized that his success was less than it could have been. Whether he had been unclear about his own personal truths or whether his personal truths had not been in harmony with those of his previous school districts, Phil recognized immediately the compatibility of his truths and those of the Fayetteville-Manlius school system.

Upon his entry into the school district, Phil took his time in fully understanding its organizational truths and the evolution of those truths over the years. The information came from stories told by staff that had been there since the school district was formed. The more he inquired and listened, the more the foundations of truth on which the district was built became clear. The board of education was clear that the community valued and needed a school system leader who led through open communication and trust. Unfortunately, there had been recent circumstances where the previous superintendent had acted in a manner that left the impression that communication and trust were not priorities. The board was specific with Phil that trust needed to be restored with it and with the community.

As he met with members of the staff and community, he heard the same call for leadership based on trust, communication, and collaboration. His mostly veteran administrative staff was emphatic about the need for a solid leadership team based on close working relationships and mutual respect. The teachers' association officers were insistent that they considered their organization a professional association, rather than a union focused on working conditions. And during his initial interactions with parent groups and community service organizations, it became obvious that open communication, respect, and trust were paramount in school-community relations. The time he invested to access the many constituents inside the school system and within the community proved invaluable. As he listened, he began to mentally internalize the association between the organization's truths and its success in academics and mutually supportive interpersonal relationships. The staff prided itself on professionalism. Consistent with his own values, Phil respected that professionalism and worked collaboratively to continue to move the district forward.

With those organizational truths and the school system's commitment to excellence and continual improvement, Phil and the staff collaboratively worked toward curriculum consistency and articulation while not insisting on lockstep instructional methodology. In addition, emphases on hiring only the best candidates and on a commitment to professional development led the district to a state of synergy where the whole became greater than the sum of its parts. Mutual respect, professionalism, collaboration, and high expectations created and sustained a culture of high morale and academic excellence.

"Who could want a better leadership environment?" Phil emphatically stated to me. Phil didn't, and he stayed there for 28 years. It is important to hear the stories, respect the history, and adapt what you learn from them to the future.

STAY FOCUSED AND GROUNDED

Depending on the history of your organization, it may be easier or more difficult to identify founding leaders and research their personal truths. The ease of such identification depends on how long the organization has been in existence and whether it is publicly or privately held, and it is also determined by other factors such as the availability of accurate information or people who may have meaningful insights. If you are not the founder of your organization, be aware that searching for the locus of energy can be a labyrinth leading to a dead end. While not an immediately satisfying outcome, it is an acceptable one because in knowing your personal truths, and having committed yourself to acting on them, you are forced to choose how to react to the dead end. Further investigation using other sources of information may be necessary. Or further self-reflection and courage may be warranted to pursue a different path than the one you are on.

Perhaps you are a leader in a large publicly held company with a long history. Its founders may have been clear on their truths and conceived the company on their purpose and passion, but they themselves are long gone. Many people since have served to shape and reshape the organization's culture. The complexity of the business as it grew may have clouded the founders' truths. Perhaps the focus on shareholder value has become primary and has become the means *and* the end. Don't despair, and don't give up on the search! Stay focused on finding the source of the Nile in your organization. Again, the point is to identify and confirm the current organizational truths flowing inside your culture so you can decide how to act on them.

As you lead your organization forward, understanding your energy and aligning it with your organization's principal truths will strengthen your leadership decision making and give you confidence to act. Just as important, it will enhance your clarity for making the significant changes necessary to adapt to new business opportunities. These business opportunities may emerge unexpectedly as that attractive resonating energy creates market gravity. Your synchronized energy serves as a solid foundation when you are challenged to lead your teams through change—and you *will* be challenged, whether it's migrating to a new ERP platform, shuttering a business unit, acquiring another company, or innovating in an unconventional way. Change is the natural state of business today in adapting to the complex and fluid global economic conditions and fast-paced competitive climate. Change "leadership" today is becoming a key competence of executive leaders, and the high-energy leaders and their supercharged organizations are positioned to win this high-stakes race.

VARIATIONS ON A THEME

The leadership experience of A. G. Lafley, former CEO of Procter & Gamble, as explained by Roger Martin in *The Opposable Mind,* serves as an excellent example. Lafley began his tenure at P&G in 1977 and worked his way through the company at various levels of responsibility. In the process, he learned, internalized, and honored the company history and the truths on which it was founded. Procter & Gamble's history dates back to 1837, and so it must have been difficult for Lafley to understand the founders and identify the organizational truths, but his resolve to learn them was not deterred.

Once upon a time, P&G was a soap and candle wax company. Then the second generation of leadership began to innovate. This generation created varieties of soap to meet differing market demands. Ivory soap was born as a result of identifying the need for an inexpensive white soap. So began P&G's long history of identifying market needs and researching and developing variations of current products or new products altogether to address those needs—a foundational truth in the P&G culture.

Lafley quickly realized the value of basing marketing decisions on extensive consumer research. Under his leadership, P&G would not launch a new product without conducting rigorous, extensive consumer testing. Unless the research for a new product clearly demonstrated its potential for substantial consumer interest, it would be doomed. This decision-making methodology and the organizational truths upon which it was based were time-honored components of the company.

Grounded with the knowledge of P&G's truths and the clarity of his own personal truths, Lafley was faced with a decision on the company's innovative development of a liquid detergent that could replace its Tide powder. Tradition tilted toward a new name. Yet Tide enjoyed enormous market share. After wrestling with the uncertain consumer response, Lafley decided to honor the value-based tradition of a new name and yet take advantage of the existing product's success. P&G called the new product Liquid Tide, and it became a runaway success.

A similar dilemma arose when P&G developed a method for compacting powdered detergent. Research involving hundreds of hand-written, voluntary consumer test responses indicated uncertainty about consumer interest, but clearly retailers would love the compact version of detergent based on the opportunity to free up shelf space. In honoring the company's long-standing practice, Lafley personally read every response and found that, while interest was not overwhelmingly enthusiastic, each response had at least one positive comment. Based on his clarity about the company's long history of relying on market research and the strong market share of its detergents, Lafley decided to move forward and approve the new product. Again, this decision proved to be an enormous success.

The leadership expertise associated with Lafley's commitment to his own personal truths, his courage and discipline to act on them, and the importance of understanding P&G's organizational truths during critical periods of change provides a clear example of the relationship between understanding those truths and leading change successfully.

SWEPT UP IN THE CURRENT

A common theme that will likely emerge as you study the history of your organization is the passion of the founders and other leaders who have shaped your culture. Invariably, you will find they were motivated by a burning purpose, and they chose to act on it. Therein lies the power of personal truths. Finding their PTs—the beliefs so important to them that they would live and die for them—the founders were prompted by inspiration into purposeful action.

Your PTs are the source of your passion. Acting on your PTs is the source of increased passion in you and in others around you. As we finish our journey upstream, we are ready to turn around and get swept up in the current. In the next chapter, we study the present-day leaders that we define as *Alpha Dogs*. I hope that you will begin to *feel* the contagiousness of their purpose and passion as you continue to feel the energy building inside you. It is this feeling of purpose and passion that provides a hint to the power of your energy as we move downstream to face the future. Ultimately, it is this feeling expressed overtly and correctly and conveyed through your powerful communication—your actions and your words— that will engage others.

Don't ignore it.

HISTORICAL TRUTHS

To function most effectively as a leader in your organization, you must clarify and understand its history, the significant stories around how it was formed, and the evolution of the organization over time. This will give you key insights into the organizational truths that have evolved over time and exist today. If you are to successfully lead your organization into the future, you must accept that change will be inevitable. However, that change must be founded on the organization's truths as well as your clarity about your own personal truths.

If you haven't done so already, talk to several long-term members of your organization. Ask them to tell you a few specific stories that would define what your organization is. Be patient and persistent, and probe with questions if necessary to understand. As you listen to the stories, go beyond the end of the story: Look for *lessons* and *themes*. Be open to many possibilities: Organizational truths may revolve around a great many themes: technical innovation, a profound customer focus, an obsession with a specific market niche, a relentless focus on cost cutting, a deep empowering of the organization's employees—you name it.

In the space provided, identify up to five *key* historical truths that you have learned are fundamental to your organization.

1. _____

2. _____

3. _____

4. _____

5. _____

Are you comfortable that these are indeed the organizational truths? If not, then identify one to three more people who are long-term members of your organization, and seek to have a dialogue with each. As before, ask them to relate at least one story about their past with the company that helped them come to value their association with it. Take time to digest each story, looking for lessons and themes. Once you have completed this activity, review your list above and identify again your organization's truths.

1. _____

2. _____

3. Now return to your personal truths as you identified them in Chapter 1. How are they consistent with the organization's truths? If they are consistent, then you and your organization clearly have the potential for a resonating, high-energy culture, and you are ready to move forward to seize the enormous potential for the success that this alignment creates. If they are not consistent, it is time for you to reflect on this revelation. What does this say about you and your organization?

_____

_____

_____

_____

_____

_____

CHAPTER 5

Pay Careful Attention to the Alpha Dog

Leadership is influence.

—JOHN C. MAXWELL, AMERICAN
AUTHOR AND PASTOR

In an October 2008 article, authors Paul B. Carroll and Chunka Mui passed along a story originally told by Harvard Business School professor Rosabeth Moss Kanter. This one will make you chuckle, but I find it a little haunting, too.

Professor Kanter once met an executive at a fabric manufacturer. New to the organization, this executive had taken over a group and managed to empower his employees by demonstrating that he was sincerely open to any new ideas. He suspected that there might be some untapped wisdom among his employees. Wisely, he created a culture in which it was not only safe but valued for lower-level employees to use their knowledge to inject energy into the organization.

Eventually, a veteran production-line worker approached the executive. He said that he had an idea that might solve a particularly annoying manufacturing problem. For years, an important type of fiber sometimes snapped during the production process. This had cost the company millions of dollars in production delays every year.

The executive heard out the idea. He immediately promised to try it out, and it worked. What a coup! Millions of dollars of savings would be realized each year. So the executive went back to the worker and said, "That was a great idea. How long have you had that idea?" "Thirty-two years," the worker responded.

Imagine that! How would it feel to be that executive? If you were that executive, would you be thrilled to strike gold by tapping the most experienced people in the organization? Or, would you be spooked by this worker's response? How many opportunities had our organization squandered over a period of decades? What other cost-cutting ideas or revenue-generating schemes had never been aired? And why? Presumably, it was because the previous executive team "knew better" than to listen to those who worked at a lower level in the organization's hierarchy.

These production workers had always reported to an authority figure at the top of an organizational chart. But we can assume that while the members of the previous executive team had authority, they apparently lacked a critical element for the ability to influence—listening—diplomatic, appreciative, and strategic listening. Leading a high-energy culture requires both a position of authority *and* the ability to influence others in order to drive economic results. When those two elements coincide—whether we're talking about the CEO, COO, CFO, CIO, CHRO, or SVP—then we are talking about an important organizational entity.

Once that fabric manufacturer created a culture in which he had built a belief that *everyone matters* as opposed to pure deference to him because of his position, a powerful business outcome emerged very quickly. He became what I like to call an Alpha Dog—a leader with position power whose behaviors create energy and drive real economic results.

People across any organizational hierarchy may have power in varying forms, all valuable. According to researchers John French and Bertram Raven, there are five types of social power:

- *Legitimate power.* The power that comes from being appointed to a position of authority

- *Coercive power.* The ability and authority to punish people for whatever reason

- *Reward power.* The ability to give people things that they might want . . . or to take away things that they might want

- *Expert power.* The power to influence through sharing knowledge, information, or expertise

▶ *Referent power.* The ability to influence others through charisma and personal acceptance

All C-suite leaders possess the first three sources of social power,
but Alpha Dogs often have expert power . . . and they *always have the
potential for* referent power. That ability to influence is what makes for a
special breed of Alpha Dog leader. These leaders provide critical insight
for us. Our goal is to identify them and observe them.

A key distinction between this next step in the process and the previous step is that now you will actually observe the subject of your investigation, the Alpha Dogs, in real time. Your focus is in the present versus
the past, and so you don't have to rely on information gleaned from other
resources. Here, you study the behaviors—including decision-making
style, communicating style, thought process, body language, and other
key observable factors—of the most influential authority figures in your
organization, today and recently. Your research in this step is primarily
observation based (see Figure 5.1).

FIGURE 5.1 | THE ENERGY CONTINUUM

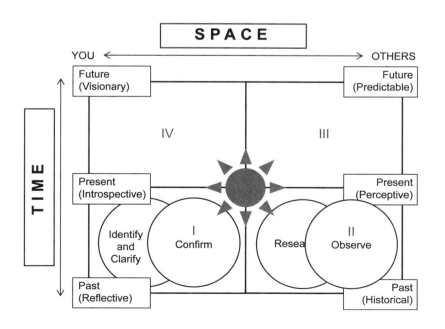

WORKING LIKE AN ALPHA DOG

The *Urban Dictionary* defines *Alpha Dog* as the leader or authority in a group, especially in a group of peers. In your business, one obvious example is the CEO or president. She is in a position of authority by virtue of title. The CEO, however, is likely not the only Alpha Dog in your organization. For our purposes here, Alpha Dogs are further defined as those leaders who are in a position of authority *and* most credible *and* those who drive consistently high-value performance. Expertise, credibility with peers, and consistent high-level results are the primary indicators of an Alpha Dog. Further, an Alpha Dog is someone who is capable of driving economic value while having the greatest positive impact on the people in your organization. Who in your organization fits this description? Is it someone besides the CEO?

The Alpha Dogs in your organization provide you with critical clues to your organization's truths. To obtain this status, their actions and behaviors must be in sync with the company's energy flow, or they would not be able to drive the value and impact the people as they do. In the case of the fabric manufacturer, for example, we could say that some issue with the company's energy flow must have kept the previous leader from developing his full power as an Alpha Dog, while the new executive came on board and created a culture that was in sync with the company's energy flow and made it happen.

*Alpha Dogs are on the same frequency as their
organization, knowingly or not.*

The very best of the breed are clear about their own personal truths, and they consciously and courageously act on them. Consequently, their leadership amplifies the existing energy of the organization and the other leaders within it.

In this chapter, we continue the process of identifying and clarifying organizational truths. Now we will add to our research the observations of present-day Alpha Dogs whose personal truths provide further insight in your quest to align your PTs with the existing flow of energy in the organization. Your efforts to identify, clarify, and confirm the personal truths of the Alpha Dogs will give you heightened potential for leveraging their energy.

MOVING THE ENERGY NEEDLE

In their book *The Talent Masters,* Bill Conaty and Ram Charan describe the opportunity Niels Fache had in observing and following the lessons he learned from Ron Nersesian, who is the president of the Electronic Measurement Group (EMG), a division of Agilent. Nersesian was vice president of the Design Validation Division, and Fache was two levels below Nersesian as a first-line manager in product planning and marketing for a variety of its businesses. He also was in charge of software product planning. Nersesian recognized Fache's potential, which permitted Fache greater access to Nersesian and the opportunity to observe and learn from him.

One area that Fache focused on improving was identifying and setting high-level strategic goals. Through observation of Nersesian's example, Fache learned quickly. Fache professes, "One thing I learned from Ron and appreciated was his strategic focus on priorities and the ability to simplify a situation to its critical parameters."

In a meeting with the company's CEO and a couple of their top executives, Fache watched carefully as Nersesian expertly painted a picture of a win-win situation, talking specifically about values, Agilent's approach to partnering with other companies, and the complementary capabilities of the two companies. It was clear to Fache that Nersesian's understanding of Agilent's culture ran deep, "and then the technical details and issues became second-order."

As Fache recalls: "It was one of my best career experiences. We had to come to an agreement with this company. Instead of getting stuck in the details, we worked out a memorandum of understanding in a two-hour meeting and dealt with the details afterward. It required around-the-clock work, but we got through it because we had this high-level agreement that became a context for the companies to work with." Fache realized the enormous value of connecting at the level of organizational truths. In this case, it was the differentiator when it came to moving the needle in the direction of a deal.

After earning a promotion to head up the mobile broadband division, Fache grew in the job, thanks to the new understanding of leadership he developed under Nersesian. Fache says, "I'm very driven and competitive, and my own synthesis guides my decision making. At the same time, I have learned a lot about the importance of relying on others and empowering leaders in the organization."

Fache paid close attention to the Alpha Dog. He observed Nersesian's own personal truths in action and connected them to his own motivation and drive. Fache is now general manager of EMG's external business development. He views Nersesian as the role model who served as the foundation of his rise through the company.

One additional and important distinction of an Alpha Dog is that she is likely to be a leader who has extraordinary communication skills. When she speaks, people listen, particularly in times of significant change or difficulty. Alpha Dogs speak with purpose and passion because their words are aligned with what is inside them. They radiate authenticity through the energy that is amplified by this alignment, and their words become powerful transmitters of their energy. When they walk into a room, they always seem to move the needle into a higher level of energy.

DRIVEN TO DRINK

Years ago, a colleague of mine completed a project for a Boston consulting firm that specialized in interviewing the top performers at companies in order to capture and bottle the behavioral competencies that differentiated them from the average employees at their organization. When reflecting on the idea of Alpha Dogs, he recalled a memorable example from those days.

A plant manager for a large beverage manufacturer didn't buy into the saying that it was lonely at the top. For him, things were lonely at the middle! This manager's personal truths revolved around his pride in cutting-edge innovation, and he wanted to overhaul the production process. Much to his frustration, he received resistance from his superiors as well as from his subordinates.

An eager student, the plant manager had been reading about the concept of just-in-time manufacturing—a new idea at that time. He knew in his bones that the concept could be applied to beverage production and that it would reap huge dividends for his company. He could create a far more flexible manufacturing process and reduce the need for warehouse space in the process.

Gradually, the plant manager won over his own people by introducing the just-in-time method in small doses. Using his expert power and referent power, he sold them on the value of the process by reminding them that they needed to be able to handle emergency or out-of-stock situations. Then the company started producing two types of beverages in one day instead of one—a previously unattainable goal. He and his team worked on decreasing the changeover times and gradually built to producing four types of beverages each day.

The manager knew that his actions were helping the company with its big-picture business goals. Inventory levels dropped dramatically, meaning that less of the company's money was tied up in capital sitting in the warehouse. Suddenly he was the best friend of the sales department, as the department was now getting a greater variety of products in a timely fashion.

Incredibly, though, senior management was not happy. The senior managers dinged him because the revamped production process caused efficiency to drop by 4 percent. The manager tried to explain that they were using a 1950s' measure of effectiveness instead of a contemporary measure, but they didn't understand. In fact, they completely *misunderstood.* They saw his costs were going down despite the fact that his efficiency was down, and so they thought he was succeeding in spite of himself! "I have to admit that I went home and needed a drink of Jack Daniels some of those days," the manager said.

Although driven to drink, he also was driven to succeed. He kept refining his process and reduced production changeover time from 20–30 minutes to 5–8 minutes. With so much less warehouse space needed, twice as many route trucks could come in each day to be filled with product. At long last, the senior managers paid attention to the Alpha Dog: They recognized their mistake . . . and they ended up sending other plant managers to learn from an old dog with a new trick. Ultimately, the whole company switched from a "just-in-case" manufacturing system to a just-in-time system.

OBSERVE WHAT ALPHA DOGS DON'T DO

As we've seen thus far in this chapter, Alpha Dogs are in positions of authority over others. But not all leaders at the top qualify as Alpha Dogs, by definition. Some individuals have "position power" and yet lack that ability to influence others. Or perhaps they *do* possess an ability to influence, but their goals are misaligned with the organization's goals. Perhaps their personal goals and truths are even absolutely contrary to the organizational mission! With that in mind, a valuable exercise would be to identify why some high-profile leaders drop out of your consideration of Alpha Dogs during this process. What behavior(s) do these people exhibit that causes you to eliminate them from consideration? Just as important, when you consider the Alpha Dogs who make the cut, what *don't* they do that keeps them in the running? What behaviors are contrary to being an Alpha Dog? Looking at these perspectives in the spirit of *dimostrazione* is extremely valuable to the art of observation, just as Leonardo da Vinci taught us.

In this light, two leaders in my past who were *not* Alpha Dogs gave me critical insight to a third, who *was*. Two of the three leaders were CEOs, and the other was a senior vice president. All three initially qualified as Alpha Dogs on the basis of authority and their ability to drive economic value into our company. All three of these high-level executives had a knack for sharing statistical information and definitive statements about our business with their audience. They all understood the value of appealing to the left brain of their important audiences—using data and metrics to support their points, which was a key lesson for me as I observed each one of their communication styles.

However, two of these leaders were cavalier with their statistics. They made troubling, bold statements when in the presence of people they believed had no way of disputing them. They would try to demonstrate a thorough grasp of the technical aspects of our business through the use of statistics, metrics, and quantified pronouncements to illustrate key points. Worse, they would influence the direction of a meeting by brashly stating one of their mistruths.

Bold communicators can be forceful leaders, but some of them have a way of "sucking all the air out of the room," a friend of mine often says.

That statement captures what it was like to be in the presence of these two senior leaders. Their confident delivery of strong statements would literally terminate further discussion and turn the direction to tactics now that their "truth" was understood. Eventually, some suspicion arose, and other leaders around the table investigated and found the statistics and statements were often off base and incorrect, even though to the unsuspecting external stakeholders they seemed real and accurate. This behavior diminished the credibility of these leaders with their colleagues.

Once I recognized this contra behavior, a behavior that ultimately proved to be countercultural, I came to appreciate the third leader more. He was always careful to clarify statistics and metrics before stating them or accepting them as truths. Through his expert use of inquiry, he always made sure the information he was receiving was accurate. He knew the decisions he would make must be founded on accurate information. More important, he knew his credibility would be at stake if he was stating something as fact that he had not verified, and he protected his credibility vigorously through "inspecting what he expected." This was a personal truth that resonated with me. As his example set the bar for our organization, credibility became recognized as being highly important to developing our leaders and as being one of the most important teaching points in our leadership development programs. "Beware of those who speak in absolutes" was how we came to describe this fatal flaw.

There are other flags to watch for as you attempt to separate the purebred Alpha Dog from the mutt who may at first glance look like the real thing. Here are some other warning signs:

▶ Failing to be self-reflective first and to own responsibility before blaming others

▶ Being more concerned with individual or political power rather than with the greater good of the organization

▶ Refusing to accept and admit mistakes

As you search for Alpha Dogs within your own organization, beware of those who use statistics and facts too often and too readily. Verify their utterances. Many technically expert leaders are clear on their statistical facts and offer them in context with confidence and integrity. Some leaders, I have come to learn, do not. In our culture, at the company where I was senior vice president of human resources, this behavior by the CEO, a true Alpha Dog, represented his personal truth that "saying what you mean and meaning what you say" is imperative, and it permeated the leadership team.

Likewise, be wary of those who also seem to need a scapegoat and never appear to acknowledge that they might have had a role in a difficulty that arose. I've found myself drawn to people who are quick to share credit and slow to point fingers without some humility and internal reflection. Leaders in high-energy cultures expect a great deal from others . . . but they expect even more of themselves. They view themselves as lifelong learners and make decisions knowing full well that some may be mistakes.

WILL POWER

Once you've identified the Alpha Dogs in your organization, it is time to study them in a way that may be unfamiliar to you. The form of study I am referring to is an art—it is a form of *curiosità*—a deeper level of observation. It is intended to create an important connection between your truths and the Alpha Dog's truths. Ultimately, by observing the connection of the Alpha Dog to the energy in the culture, you serve to connect your energy to the culture as well (see Figure 5.2).

The actor Will Smith has said he searches relentlessly for the one thing that connects him to the character he is portraying. This single connection provides a conduit to "becoming" this person, assuming the persona of the character, and channeling the energy of the real person through himself so that he "is" that person on screen. As an example, Smith connected to Muhammad Ali through Ali's moral code and political views and Ali's legendary courage to stand up for what he believes. For instance, Ali was arrested because he declared himself a conscientious objector to the war in Vietnam—well before this was a popular stance. As a result, his boxing license was suspended, and he was stripped of his title. A lengthy legal battle dragged on until public opinion on the war turned in his favor, allowing him to resume his career.

FIGURE 5.2 | PERSONAL TRUTHS PYRAMID

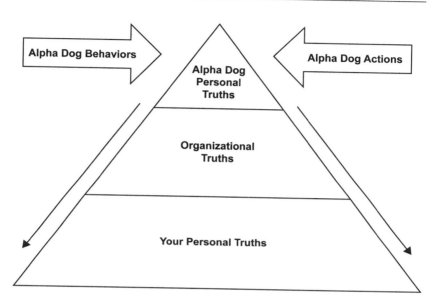

Smith's own moral code is similarly grounded in a personal truth from his youth, namely the relationship (or lack thereof) with his father. Smith courageously speaks out about the role black men should play in the lives of their children and families. As trite as it may seem, a scene from Smith's old television show *The Fresh Prince of Bel-Air*, where Smith's character's biological father rejects him by jilting him on a planned father-son trip, is a powerful example. Will's connection to that character came from a deeply seated, past experience with his own father. The scene, most of it unscripted, demonstrates the power of the connective energy between Will, his character, and his personal truth. Connecting to the Alpha Dog in your organization on the level of personal truths will have a similar impact on you as a leader.

If you have selected your Alpha Dogs carefully, they will be extremely valuable to your development as an energized leader. Your observation of the behaviors and actions of these exemplary leaders will connect you with them in a way that will give you further insight into your connection to the existing flow of energy in your organization.

CHAMPIONSHIP-CALIBER ALPHA DOGS

Perhaps there is no better example of the value of an energized culture than a successful NFL football franchise. An NFL team's performance is as much a business challenge as it is a lesson in leadership, teamwork, talent selection, preparation, practice, work ethic, and many other factors that correlate to business success. The best coaches become the best because they study and coach with Alpha Dogs, who have *that something special* that influences those around them.

Mike Holmgren is currently the president of the Cleveland Browns and one of the most highly regarded coaches in the NFL. He won a championship with the Green Bay Packers in Super Bowl XXXI and brought a second team, the once perennially mediocre Seattle Seahawks, to a Super Bowl. Mike Holmgren will tell you that he was fortunate to have coached under the legendary Bill Walsh, head coach of the San Francisco 49ers. Walsh's nickname "The Genius" was a result of his team's unparalleled dominance during the late 1980s—six division titles, three NFC Championship titles, and three Super Bowl titles. Bill Walsh's genius as a coach—he's credited with creating the innovative West Coast offense—is only outdone by his genius as a leader who developed other successful leaders like Dennis Green, Mike Shanahan, George Seifert, Paul Hackett, and Holmgren.

It has been said that leadership excellence is not a function of how many people you lead; rather it is a function of how many great leaders you develop. Mike Holmgren studied his Alpha Dog, Bill Walsh. He learned that Bill Walsh's personal truth was finding talent that fit his system—perfectly. Walsh sought players who were considered unconventional for their positions in the NFL at the time, but skilled in the area they needed to excel for purposes of driving results. His system was only a competitive advantage if the players gave the system a differentiating advantage. In the area of talent management, this gave Walsh a slight advantage because he could trade down for a lower pick in the draft and still get the players who would fit his system and give his strategy life. Walsh also believed the head coach should be the primary decision maker when selecting players. Above his sixth sense for talent, Walsh's predominant PTs were pride and dignity, and he instilled them so deeply into the culture that they remain part of the San Francisco 49er franchise today.

To Mike Holmgren, Bill Walsh was an Alpha Dog in every sense. To go along with Holmgren's own success as a coach and leader, the list of great leaders he's developed is equally impressive—Jon Gruden, Marty Mornhinweg, Andy Reid, and Ray Rhodes to name a few, all great coaches in their own right. Holmgren observed Walsh well, connected to him, and now extends that connection to his own protégés, teams, and the business that is the Cleveland Browns.

If you're more of a baseball fan, another notable Alpha Dog would be Hall of Fame pitcher Nolan Ryan. The flame-throwing pitcher is a legend because of his amazing records with strikeouts and no-hitters, but here's a statistic that is even more telling: A total of 11 of Ryan's former teammates have named a child either "Nolan" or "Ryan" in his honor. That speaks volumes for how admired he was as a teammate, likely in large part due to his combination of an amazing work ethic and his grounded humility.

Ryan attributes his values to his dad. His father worked for an oil company but delivered the *Houston Post* every morning, often with Nolan at his side. "Dad worked two jobs to put four girls through college," Ryan has said. "I know he didn't want to get up at one in the morning, but that's what he had to do, so he did it. I think that's why I am the way I am."

Not surprisingly, Ryan has moved into a leadership role as the CEO and principal owner of the Texas Rangers, a franchise that failed to make the playoffs in its first 24 years and then failed to advance beyond the first round in its first three postseason appearances. With Ryan at the helm, that has changed. According to ESPNDallas.com, he set a goal of 92 wins in 2010; the team won 90 and ended up making it to the World Series. In 2011, the goal was 90 to 95 wins, and the team won 96 games and its second consecutive American League Championship. Ryan's energizing leadership is clearly having an impact.

THE TOP DOGS

For their book *Lessons from the Top*, Thomas J. Neff and James M. Citrin studied the best-performing organizations over the previous decade and determined the CEO most responsible for the company's success during that time. Their selection methodology gave them a candidate pool of 240 CEO leaders, from which they selected the 50 best at the time, including Michael Dell of Dell Computer, John Chambers of Cisco Systems, Howard Schultz of Starbucks, and Jack Welch of General Electric.

Their objective was to find and study the very best business leaders to determine the common factors that made them great. Their conclusion: "The greatest success is achieved when a leader of an organization is consistent, when the organization is consistent, and when this consistency is linked to what the company stands for and how it behaves." I have been fortunate to experience an organization that embodies Neff and Citrin's definition of greatness.

In our fast-growing retail furniture organization, we were fortunate to have several leaders who qualified as Alpha Dogs. As I mentioned in Chapter 1, Neil Goldberg, the CEO of Raymour & Flanigan and my boss when I worked for that company, was one of them. Sure, he had the legitimate power and reward power that most bosses have. But he also had the referent power that makes someone a true leader and an Alpha Dog. His humility and charisma, his candor and consistency, made him a veritable power plant of energy. If you wanted to understand how Raymour & Flanigan could thrive in troubled times, you had to start by paying attention to him.

Now it is time to identify your Alpha Dogs with the intent of connecting their personal truths to your own. As you capture the truths the Alpha Dogs demonstrate through their actions, words, and behaviors, you should have a moment of epiphany where the connection becomes real—the connection to you and to your organization. This is critical. In the next chapter, we'll check the accuracy of your definition of the organizational truths with the sources that matter most—the people in your organization who best understand the truths that are currently in play.

Alpha Dog Analysis (ADA)

In Chapter 4, we focused on discovering the historical truths of the organization and those of its founder(s), and perhaps other leaders along the way who helped shape them. The premise is that there is an existing energy in the organization that these leaders helped create, just as there is an innate energy in each of us that must be identified, clarified, and confirmed. Aligning our own personal truths with the organization's truths gives us the potential for resonance.

Here in Chapter 5, we have turned our attention to present-day leaders, the key decision makers we affectionately call the Alpha Dogs of your organization. Alpha Dogs are the one, two, or three key leaders in your organization with position authority, current or recently, who have driven the most economic value while having the greatest positive impact on the people in your organization. They also have credibility with their peers and with everyone in the organization.

In the space provided, identify the person or people you have deemed Alpha Dogs in your organization:

Alpha Dog #1 _____

Alpha Dog #2 _____

Alpha Dog #3 _____

Now that you've identified them, take a few moments to think and answer the following questions for each Alpha Dog:

What are key words and phrases you hear them say often?

_____

_____

When forced to prioritize, what choices do they make?

_____

_____

What behaviors do you witness when they're at their very best?

_____

_____

How do they behave in times of crisis?

_____

_____

What is their decision-making style?

_____

_____

What is their communication style?

_____

_____

What don't they do, ever?

_____

_____

What upsets them?

_____

_____

What excites them?

_____

_____

How do you feel when you are around them?

_____

_____

Are their behaviors consistent? If not, what is inconsistent? What stimulates the inconsistency?

_____

_____

If you had to boil down their most important truth to a short phrase, what would you say?

_____

_____

Now reflect on your answers above. What personal truths emerge in your mind for the Alpha Dogs as you see them portrayed in their actions? Capture those personal truths in writing.

1. _____

2. _____

3. _____

4. _____

5. _____

CONNECTING PTS

The next element of this exercise may prove most valuable. Return to your answers for the exercise in Chapter 4 and compare the Alpha Dogs' personal truths with the organization's core values. How consistent are they? List the consistent truths here.

_____

_____

_____

_____

_____

What excites you about these consistencies?

_____

_____

_____

If your PTs are connected with the organization's values and with the PTs of the Alpha Dogs within your organization, great—you and your organization are poised for success! If they are not consistent, then it is time to search within yourself as to the consequence, and you should begin to consider the options you have to remain true to your PTs.

CHAPTER 6

Query the Key Players

> *You're the one who sees the truth, the Prajna (to use a Tibetan word), in a situation. Once you see the truth in a situation you know how to navigate it. You have the guts to navigate it. You care enough to navigate it.*
>
> —SETH GODIN, AMERICAN ENTREPRENEUR,
> AUTHOR, AND SPEAKER

Have you ever watched a CBS TV show called *Undercover Boss*? The premise is that a senior executive of a large company goes "undercover" by taking a low-level position within his own organization. The person adopts an alias, alters his appearance, and is given a fictional history. No one in the organization knows that this is actually the CEO of the whole organization. The intriguing part is what the CEO ends up learning about his organization. Will the surprises be pleasant or unpleasant?

In October 2010, Mike White, chairman, president, and CEO of DirecTV, posed as a trainee at his own company. Although White had 20 years of experience working with products such as Pepsi and Doritos, he was relatively new to the communications industry. He took the challenge as an opportunity to learn how employees *really* performed in their own element—as opposed to how they might react if "the CEO" paid a visit amid much fanfare. It was an opportunity to get an unfiltered view of what was really going on as opposed to a perspective that might be spun by middle managers who might worry what the big boss would learn.

In this case, White was deeply moved by the caring and commitment of the installer, logistics manager, and customer service representative who "trained" him. And his unpleasant surprises reflected badly more on the company than on the people: His installers had been forced to buy their own GPS systems to locate customers' houses. The installers also were undermined and delayed by software that loaded too slowly. And he also found that the company could do more to help employees reach their personal development goals.

The upshot is that *Undercover Boss* gives executives a chance to get out of their lonely if elegant castles and thrusts them alongside those who are cleaning out the moat or polishing the armor. It's by no means a new story. In Shakespeare's *Henry V*, the great king disguises himself on the eve of a great battle to find out what his soldiers *really* think of him . . . and he finds that some harbor doubts, leaving him to lament the isolation of power.

THE UNTOLD STORY

Do you remember the scene in *A Few Good Men*, where an officer angrily shouts, "You can't *handle* the truth"? More leaders would be wise to be haunted about what they might not know. What untold stories exist in your organization, and how might you alter your course if you learned what the key stakeholders *really* think about your company and your leadership style?

If you have ever been part of an organization where the values are prominently displayed in framed posters on every wall, yet the employees ignore them, or worse, the atmosphere is one in *direct conflict* with the stated values, then you already understand the importance of querying the key players.

> *Your organization's truths are understood best by those who function daily within its atmosphere—your employees, your customers, your vendors.*

These are the people who make your organization tick every day. Who is talking to them? How do you ensure that you're getting the straight story?

This next step in our process will explain how to understand the "actual" truths in play within your organization from the viewpoint of these, and other, key stakeholders. As with the Alpha Dogs, your perspective here is an external one, meaning it is focused on others, not you. But different from the process in the last chapter, you will depend less on observation and more on conclusions drawn from creating an effective, intentional *dialogue* with these stakeholders. The intention is to understand how *they* view the organization's truths when *you* listen deeply, without bias. To do this, you will use a method called "dynamic inquiry," a concept introduced by Chris Argyris in his book *Flawed Advice and the Management Trap*. Dynamic inquiry is defined as "a process of interacting with other people in a conversation that is diplomatic, appreciative, and strategic. It requires practice and presence in order to work at a level which is actionable."

Since this is an external versus internal perspective with an emphasis on actively understanding the real and potentially unflattering truths that exist within your organization, we have now moved to the upper right quadrant of the resonating energy continuum shown in Figure 6.1.

FIGURE 6.1 | THE ENERGY CONTINUUM

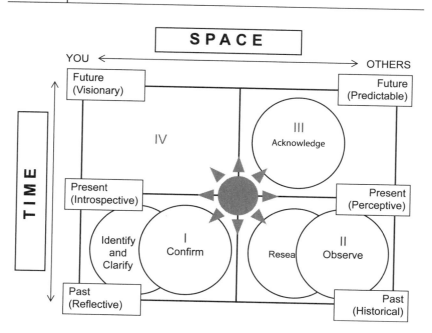

Learning what your employees, customers, and vendors know will open your mind to new ways to leverage the truths in play for the benefit of each of these constituents and for the business. You will view things differently. In the spirit of *dimostrazione*, you will have gained wisdom from multiple viewpoints that will challenge or confirm your own. That's simply another form of acid test. You will have mitigated any risk of false conclusions while at the same time prompting your own thoughts toward a course of action that would have otherwise been left unconsidered. Your resonating energy will increase as you see, hear, and feel the energy of your truths in others, particularly as they describe the truths in your organization. You will become more energized as the leader of an organization that has your truths embedded in its culture.

THE FOUR PHASES

As a leader, you will reap significant adjunct benefits from this often-overlooked step in the process of creating and sustaining a high-resonance, high-energy organization. As you understand the depth of engagement and learn how to have meaningful and effective dialogue with your employees, you will consequently acknowledge their value and empower them. Your credibility will increase as their understanding of your defined personal truths becomes clearer to them. You will take steps to becoming a more authentic leader. The four-phase process described here and in the next three chapters is outlined in Figure 6.2.

Phase 1. Acknowledgment

With the acknowledgment phase, you are seeking to admit to yourself and accept the reality of the current truths at work in your organization. As with wedding vows, this admission must be for better or worse! Your actions here, when sincere, express recognition. This is why this step begins with your employees.

Why does what your employees think matter? Let me share a story from my days creating the Leadership Development Institute at Raymour & Flanigan. When we were framing the structure of our leadership development curriculum, our extensive research led us to conclude

FIGURE 6.2 | THE FOUR A'S PROCESS

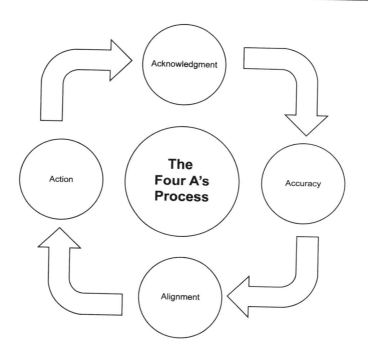

that building effective leaders organically was clearly a function of clarity of "values"—both those that are personal to the leaders and those that are germane to the organization. We set out to create a curriculum that effectively explained the reasons for this conclusion, so that the leaders we developed would understand the importance of clarifying values. The curriculum would include:

▶ Theory that confirmed the importance of clarity of both types of values

▶ Real-time examples of the theory in action with current leaders in our organization

▶ A series of creative, interactive exercises that would help our "students" clarify their own personal values and their perception of the organization's values

One such interactive exercise nearly derailed the whole program in the first year. This problematic exercise was called the "Value Wheel."

WHEEL OF MISFORTUNE

Unlike the exercises that were part of the program's personal values segment, the Value Wheel was designed to confirm what my project colleagues and I had already concluded were the organization's values. In hindsight, this was a foolish and possibly even arrogant conclusion.

My colleagues and I worked diligently to identify our organizational values during the development phase of the institute. We solicited input from the owners, the founder, and people at every level of the organization. We incorporated observations from several different perspectives. For instance, I had been with the company for five years at the time, and my role took me to every nook and cranny of the organization. I worked hand-in-hand with the owners themselves. My partner in this project, Holly, our director of people development, had been with the company only a short time but interacted with many people on our campus and had a keen observational ability. Phil, the third key project team member, was a vendor to us but very familiar with the organization. He had lived and worked in the same city where the company was founded and headquartered for more than 40 years. His informed "external" perspective was very useful. The three of us actively and systematically solicited and captured input from others within the organization.

When we finally began to organize our collective conclusions on the organization's values, each of us had very strong opinions. Accordingly, we began to debate. After some time, we had an epiphany about a creative way to organize the results—thus, the birth of the Value Wheel. We had concluded that the values fell into differing categories around our core mission as a company, "To Enhance the Customer's Shopping Experience." We decided that the values we identified within our culture should be organized in rings around this core central mission. The rings included our employees' values, our leaders' values, and our organization's values. The end product of this epiphany is displayed in Figure 6.3.

We were very proud of what we had created. We then decided that we would create a group exercise to be used as an evening activity during the first week of the three-week class. The first week was intense and

FIGURE 6.3 | THE VALUE WHEEL

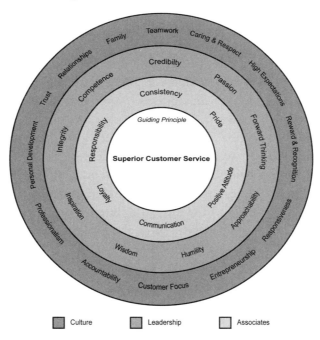

Organizational Characteristics and Core Values

designed to "break down" our leaders. To focus them, we felt it important to humble them constructively. First, we wanted to ensure that they truly understood the principles of leadership. Then we wanted to test their clarity of values using videotape. It was quite effective. While viewing their own answers to "What are your personal values?" the leaders could see that they created a house of cards. They needed to construct a more solid foundation of personal truths. Once focused, these people worked to become better leaders, collaborating and building relationships with other leaders from around the company. The mix served to help open the minds of all.

For the evening exercise, we created breakout groups that represented a diverse mix of leaders encompassing a variety of levels, geographic locations, genders, and tenures with the company. It was fascinating to facilitate and observe the interaction of the eclectic groups.

Without divulging our own Value Wheel to the class, we challenged the participants to agree on the organization's values and then later present them to the larger group. We gave them a blank Value Wheel diagram, a set of very simple guidelines, and a two-hour time limit.

As the first class returned to the main room for the presentations, my colleagues and I were energized with excitement. We couldn't wait to see the groups confirm what we already knew! Yet when the first group began to present, it was clear that the group members had identified organizational values that were not even on our list! Further, they had quickly discounted two we had confidently identified as absolute values. I'm not sure what the expressions on our faces were, but I know that we were so bewildered, we were rendered speechless. Somehow we got through the three group presentations that evening, but we were completely thrown by the results. These 18 people from every corner and level of the organization had identified different values from the ones we had carefully determined. Moreover, the three groups' conclusions did not appear to agree with one another. *Wow!* "What now?" we asked ourselves.

Ultimately, we decided to continue with the exercise and observe what each of the next six classes concluded about the organization's values. It turned out to be a very good decision. We learned that the diverse opinions were not isolated to the first group, nor were they a function of poor direction. We learned our presumed conclusions simply were not valid. More important, we learned that within almost every group, there was a set of common-denominator values emerging.

Then, during an internal speaking engagement where our CEO was addressing a group of bankers, Holly had another epiphany. Our CEO's description of the organization's values—in his very words and phrasing—was consistent with the common values our diverse employee groups had identified. Bingo! We had finally captured and clarified our organization's values. Using our CEO's words, they became known as:

- ▶ Walk the Talk
- ▶ Raise the Bar
- ▶ Be One Team

We learned that our employees' perceptions of the organization's values were different from ours. However, through intensive dialogue, listening, and patience, we were able to find the common ground and ultimately discover the organizational values that were already clear to our employees.

The process of acknowledgment had led us to the reality of our organization's truths. Along the way, we created enormous employee buy-in because we expressly solicited and recognized the input from our most important resource, our people.

What do your employees know? What do they believe? How do they describe your organization? Do you truly know *their* reality? It's unlikely you'll have the good fortune to run a yearlong project similar to ours to find out. Yet whether you do so on your own or with the help of your HR team or communications consultants, it is critical that you understand what your employees really think. This builds trust and creates buy-in once you have clarified their input.

So how does "acknowledgment" happen efficiently and effectively, particularly in the absence of an exercise like the Value Wheel? How do you solicit meaningful input from your employees? The answer is through dynamic inquiry.

Phase 2. Accuracy through Dynamic Inquiry

Accurate conclusions are imperative if we are to realize the economic value of aligning organizational truths with our own PTs. Our value wheel exercise, though serendipitous at the time, did exactly this when we queried diverse groups of our employees to verify what we thought we already knew. The result was enlightening and caused us to rethink our conclusions. Similarly, querying the key players in your organization in a way that gets to the core of their reality will serve to verify or discount the accuracy of your conclusions. By creating opportunities for others to take the lead in discussions and interactions, dynamic inquiry helps to discover deeper meaning more efficiently than linear questioning and dialogue do. Rather than seeking information through the more standard, highly linear interactive process of employee surveys, dynamic inquiry is a relational interaction that seeks to benefit from a mutually determined and open-ended line of questions and answers.

A good example of dynamic inquiry took place during our interaction with our leaders during the classroom portion of their development. To put the leaders in the right frame of mind to reflect on their perception of the organization's values, we used an approach that required them to stretch their imaginations. We asked them to imagine themselves at a family picnic with relatives, young and old—but people they see only rarely. There is food, drink, and music, and it is a beautiful, sunny summer day. The atmosphere is one of joyful reunion. You chat with loved ones you have not seen since another family gathering—maybe a wedding. You sit down to eat next to a favorite cousin you've missed, and he asks you what you are doing now. You tell him.

At this point we created a mock dialogue between the leader and his "cousin." During the mock dialogue we would ask, "Tell me what your organization is like." The person might respond that it is a very good company with a lot of opportunity. The conversation might continue this way:

"I'm a store manager in Poughkeepsie."

"What's it like working there?"

"Well, it's a very high-expectation environment."

"Really? What does that mean?"

"I'm expected to deliver certain performance metrics weekly against a budget."

"Hmmm. Sounds intense."

"Yes, but it's also very team oriented, so I feel like I have good support around me from operations and customer care."

"So you like the team?"

"Yes, very much. We work closely together and support each other. We are working toward a common goal, but we respect each other's areas of responsibility."

With role-playing dialogue like this, now you are getting to the core of how employees view the organization. You need to listen carefully to the words and phrases the leader uses to describe his work when speaking to a layperson. In the preceding dialogue, we heard things like "high expectations," "team," "support," and "respect," all hints of the current truths of the organization.

As he conceives relationships within an organization, social scientist and business theorist Chris Argyris believes that the words individuals use and the behavior they exhibit are based on two "theories of action." When asked about their organization, these individuals know what the *expected* ways of responding are. These are what Argyris calls the "espoused theory." These individuals are saying or doing what is expected of them to say or do. However, they also have another set of personal, internal rules or mind maps that are indicative of what they more deeply think or feel. This is a "theory-in-use."

Both are theories of action, because different situations can prompt different ways of responding. In one case, a member of an organization will say or behave in a manner consistent with the organization's expectations. He is being loyal to the organization. In another case, he will say or behave in a manner consistent with a different, more personal set of beliefs or feelings.

The importance for us is whether there is *congruence* between the two theories. For example, in explaining his actions to a colleague, an individual may call upon some convenient piece of the espoused theory. He might explain to others, or to himself at some level, his sudden rush out of the office by saying he had to go "fight fires" on behalf of a colleague. Sometimes employees throw around such business buzzwords to disguise or exaggerate the importance of their actions.

When our words and our actions are consistent with those expected in our culture, congruence exists. Mark K. Smith, Rank Research Fellow and a specialist in the field of informal education, explains that "much of the business of supervision, where it is focused on the practitioner's thoughts, feelings, and actions, is concerned with the gulf between espoused theory and theory-in-use, or in bringing the latter to the surface. This gulf is not necessarily bad. However, if it gets too wide, then there is clearly a difficulty. But provided the two remain connected, the gap creates an opportunity for meaningful dialogue."

Therefore, to get at what an employee *really* thinks, you might want to use dynamic inquiry, a very useful technique.

Employing dynamic inquiry effectively during this step in the process generates other benefits, including the ability to mitigate "fantasy risk." This is the risk associated with defining organizational values based on the fantasies of an individual—maybe the CEO or the head of HR—or a group (the executive team or a team tasked with defining the corporate values) rather than reality. Our bold, almost arrogant conclusions about our company values that led to the creation of the value wheel is an example of "fantasy risk" in real time. Here's another example without naming names: Someone I know told me about a growing organization that has a rampant turnover problem. This company employs dozens of low-level employees who have extremely large loads of clients they must support over the phone. The issues are complex and emotional, and many of these employees spend most of their day helping clients wade through bureaucracy.

Even in a bad economy where unemployment is high, this company was seeing turnover numbers well over 30 percent. This proved extremely costly in terms of morale, let alone in terms of all the effort that had to go into continual recruiting and training. Yet upper management refused to overhaul the ways in which entry-level employees were hired and trained. Why? The executive team clung to the fantasy that younger-generation workers lacked a sense of commitment to their work and were not loyal to any organization. The team took a "like it or lump it" attitude to the problem instead of reflecting critically on what the constant exodus said about the organization. And so the revolving door continues to spin.

Fantasy risk carries significant consequences without the insurance of offsetting the potentially negative impacts. A significant consequence of promoting "fantasy" organizational values is lower trust between the workers and management. Misaligned truths, where employees feel management says one thing and does another, are detrimental to the organization's health and welfare. Energy becomes dampened, and the existing energy in such cultures is quieted.

Leaders who actively seek input through periodic, meaningful dialogue with their employees build trust and credibility with their people which in turns builds capacity for the free flow of powerful energy within the organization. We'll describe how to leverage this atmosphere for the free flow of powerful energy in Chapter 8, but building capacity increases the potential economic value of this principle. In her book *Discover Your CEO Brand*, Suzanne Bates recalls coaching the CIO of the largest division of a major financial services firm. "This leader was widely admired and well-known for his brand values. I worked with his entire team, so I can tell you from personal interviews and experience that *every single one of his direct reports, every one of their directs, and the next layer down*, could all tell you the three words that were important to their success—three words that happened to define this leader's brand. He lived his brand, talked about the values, and encouraged others to live them. Not surprisingly, his team vastly outperformed all others in that function across the company.

"Why was he so successful? First, he focused on communicating with his own team. They soon were able to talk about and act on those values. After a while, they became very good at communicating them as well. As a high-performing team, they constantly referred to these values, and also talked about how much they admired the leader. His team knew what he stood for, respected him, and saw the power of those ideas and values in making them successful. They adopted his way and measured themselves against it. But it all began because he knew himself, knew what he stood for, and knew how to communicate to others."

THE IMPORTANT HIDDEN VALUE

Acknowledging and confirming the accuracy of key players' perceptions deepens relationships with your people while it strengthens your leadership brand. It promotes synchronicity with your truths as your resonating energy ignites the innate energy of all the people you touch. The truths you speak and act on will attract and resonate with the truths your employees believe and know are real in your organization. That's the power of resonating energy at work.

J. Willard Marriott, Jr., the legendary CEO and chairman of Marriott International, Inc., says, "Energy is probably the most important thing in a CEO." In his global lodging company, Marriott relentlessly pursues customer satisfaction and believes Marriott's employees drive success, creating a culture of service that differentiates the company from its competition. To ensure he understands what his employees know, he walks the properties and engages in a meaningful dialogue with people at all levels of the organization. When he engages, he is appreciative and diplomatic, yet strategic. He says: "Honesty is just paramount. People have to trust a CEO. They've got to know he walks the talk, or she walks the talk. They've got to know the CEO believes in something besides profits. We try and foster a very strong belief in the importance of the individual and the importance of our people. We think profits are important, but they're not as important as the individual."

Similarly, other important stakeholders understand the truths of your organization and should be sought out for their insights and acknowledged. Certainly, you already understand the importance of customers to your success and to your business's success. But do you really know how your customers view your organization? What do your customers "know" about your organization? What do they believe? How do they describe your organization? These same questions apply to vendors and investors. The realities of your organization's truths are known by each of these constituencies. Understanding what they perceive is important to drawing your own accurate conclusions about the truths currently at work in your culture.

Why is this so important? What is the economic opportunity, or conversely, the opportunity cost? Employees want work that is aligned with their values. Studies confirm that such alignment creates self-motivation. Marketing is becoming more difficult because it is becoming more listening oriented than telling oriented. That's the secret that undergirds the success of Twitter—and of the business leaders who understand the use of social media as a marketing tool. Increasingly, companies are watching and listening to their customers individually. Business leaders who truly engage people—employees, customers, vendors, investors—and listen to and learn from their truths will flourish. They will be the leaders who drive enormous economic value into their business and stomp the competition.

The culture of business is shifting dynamically. The Internet and mobile electronics are changing every aspect of our organizational lives. Connecting with individuals is more important than ever, at least partly because it is now so incredibly easy and fast to do so.

THE NEED TO DIG FOR THE GOLD

As you inquire and listen carefully and purposefully to what individuals or members of a group are saying and as you clarify what you hear, a tautology will emerge. A tautology is a repetition of words or phrases that are largely insignificant. Most processes of inquiry stop once answers are given. They capture the words and phrases that are oft repeated and hold them as truths. This is a missed opportunity. Your task is to find the truth *behind* the tautology—the gold that is hidden beneath the surface.

For those in the creative design domain, this is much like the concept of "mind mapping," a process of using a diagram to organize and link ideas around a central concept. Beginning with the central concept, a mind map progressively branches outward to other associated concepts or ideas. Starting from the central concept, several related branches of thinking are represented graphically. The process helps you explore the full scope of possibilities related to the original, central concept.

What you do with the information you have gathered is the next key step in the process of querying the players. You may choose to dispute, rationalize, or even discount the truths you have learned are the perceptions of your employees, vendors, and customers. This is dangerous. You have to be able to handle the truth. Disputing, discounting, downplaying, rationalizing, and ignoring will prevent you from acting on these truths. It also diminishes the value of acknowledging their significance. Worse, it can weaken or even destroy the trust built during the process, diminishing your credibility with the very people you lead. At its worst, this can be like the human relations approach of the 1960s, in which organizations sometimes solicited input to make people *feel* involved without necessarily acting on the input.

You may try to change people's perception of reality, convincing them that their views are off the mark. This, too, is a dangerous tack. Attempting to change perceptions actually increases the odds that you will be seen as a leader who is out of touch. Acceptance will do more to drive you and your organization forward. Don't fall into the trap of focusing on questioning the perceptions of others or attempting to change them. Focusing on the truths that are consistent with your own is the secret to success.

THE DYNAMIC INQUIRY PROCESS

Now that we've talked about why you need to query the key players and what might result, let's dig in to how you actually go about digging beneath the surface for that gold.

As you approach a dynamic inquiry opportunity, recognize that the essence of the activity is about the other person—not you. You want to gather information that lies beneath the surface of knee-jerk espoused theory. Recall the three significant dimensions of dynamic inquiry: It must be *diplomatic, appreciative*, and *strategic*.

While the focus is on the other individual, you are the key to its success. The inquiry process requires careful listening and thinking on your part. As much as reasonably possible, you have to block out your own personal perspectives, mindset, and preconceived notions about the individual and about his responses. You are on a "search, record, and learn" mission only.

As you proceed with the dynamic inquiry, pay careful attention to the individual's response. Carefully record the responses either mentally, in writing, or ideally on a digital voice recorder. Make judgments about where to take the path of inquiry as you continue forward.

For example, let's imagine that you're starting with one of your employees. You will then proceed to a second and possibly third employee, then to customers, vendors, and, perhaps, investors. Remember, the skill you are developing here is essential to your development as a leader.

Your approach to this activity with an employee may be direct or indirect. For a direct approach, you may inform the employee that you would like to know and understand his impression of the company or organization. You have three or four questions you would like to ask that would only take a few minutes. Or the circumstances may be right for you to extend a conversation with the employee that began with a different purpose. Here you just add the same path of inquiry without specifically explaining your purpose.

I suggest opening the inquiry with one or two benign questions, such as "How long have you been associated with the company or organization?" followed by "What *attracted* you originally to the company or organization?" Customize these suggestions to the individual, understanding that the initial questions should be benign enough to put the employee at ease.

Then follow with questions like these:

▶ "What is it like working here?"

▶ "What do you consider to be the strengths of our company or organization?"

Your reaction to the employee's response must be accepting and acknowledging. Don't show surprise or disappointment. Rather you should convey interest in the employee's response. Remember your first role here is as a listener, not as a judge.

As you consider the response or responses you have heard, reflect on them and then *carefully* frame the next question. It should reflect your interest, and yet it should not directly guide the person's thinking. You may respond, "Really, what does that mean?" Or you may say, "I'm interested in your response. Tell me a little more" or "Could you give me an example?" *The pivotal point here is to invite the key player to think more deeply about his response, to ask him to dig deeper into his thinking and feelings, providing more detail.*

As you record the individual's responses, reach beneath all the extraneous words and phrases for the essence of the response. Continue with the inquiry until you feel you truly have reached and understood the deeper thinking or feeling of the individual about the company or organization.

Here are some additional possible questions:

▶ "How would you describe this organization's mission or purpose?"

▶ "What are some words you might use to describe what the company stands for?"

▶ "What does the organization value above all else, from your perspective?"

Along the way, you should guide the interaction to prompt the individual to provide an explanation of his thinking or feeling to ensure that, indeed, it is accurate. Remember the possible tautology here. People may be inclined to toss out words just to be responsive, and they may be inclined to express what they think you want to hear—the "company line." Thus, you need to politely pursue the inquiry with genuine interest until you feel that the individual has reached the stage of providing accurate and "real" thinking and opinions. Remember to make the person continue to feel comfortable and appreciated.

After the interaction is finished, immediately make written notes about the responses if you haven't recorded them. While it would be important to try to capture all that the person said, it is critical to record the essence of its deeper meaning.

In the next chapter, we will focus on the next of the four A's—alignment. We will show you how to align with the common truths you've learned from your key players so your resonating energy is amplified. And in Chapter 8, we focus on the final and perhaps most important A—action. Congratulations! Now you are nearing the three-quarter mark in the process of creating a high-energy culture.

DYNAMIC INQUIRY

The exercises in Chapters 1, 2, and 3 required you to do deep personal thinking about yourself. The exercises in Chapters 4 and 5 asked you to think and make judgments about your organization, its founder(s), its legacy, and the Alpha Dogs you have identified and observed. You have gathered significant insights by exploring your thinking both internally and externally. With this exercise, you will extend that external search for meaning much more deftly. You will practice and develop your dynamic inquiry skills.

For some of you, this may be a simple extension of a skill you already possess. For others, however, this may be a new or challenging, but most meaningful, activity that will surely develop your leadership skills and provide enormous value to your growth as a leader.

If necessary, review the process that was described at the end of this chapter. Then complete the steps in the sample worksheet. The second worksheet is a blank model you can use with any set of questions.

Sample Dynamic Inquiry Worksheet: Name (for an employee)

Inquiry #1 How long have you been associated with our company (or organization)?

Response #1

Inquiry #2 *(Choose one.)* What is it like working here? What do you consider to be the strengths of our company (or organization)?

Response #2

Inquiry #3 *(Choose one.)* Really, what does that mean? I'm interested in your response. Tell me a little more. Could you give me an example?

Response #3

Inquiry #4 *Customize a question here to go deeper into capturing what this individual believes to be true about your organization's missions, values, and priorities.*

Response #4

Dynamic Inquiry Worksheet: Name

_____

Inquiry #1 _____

Response #1

_____

_____

Inquiry #2 _____

Response #2

_____

_____

Inquiry #3 _____

Response #3

_____

_____

Inquiry #4 _____

Response #4

_____

_____

Once you have completed your first experience (and feel more comfortable with the process), select one or two more employees and repeat the process. When you have finished these inquiries, pursue a similar dynamic inquiry opportunity with two or three customers or vendors.

Remember that you not only are gathering important information but also are honing your leadership skills. Here you might begin with simple, comfortable questions such as "How long have you purchased from our company?" or "How long have you provided products or services to our company?" You may follow with "What about the company or organization initially attracted you to us?" Then dig deeper with "What do you consider to be our company's strengths or advantages?" or something similar, depending on the relationship. When you have crossed this bridge, then follow the same path of inquiry as you did with employees. Once finished, remember to make written notes.

Finally, if possible, do the same with investors, for here you may literally find the gold beneath the surface. Use the model Dynamic Inquiry Worksheet as often as necessary.

CHAPTER 7

Crack the Code to Your "Secret Sauce"

Everything that can be counted does not necessarily count;
everything that counts cannot necessarily be counted.

—ALBERT EINSTEIN, THEORETICAL
PHYSICIST AND NOBEL PRIZE WINNER

In 1866, John Pemberton created "Merchandise X," the secret formula for Coca-Cola. Decades later, company president Robert W. Woodruff astutely built a publicity, marketing, and intellectual property strategy around that closely guarded recipe.

And so it remains, apparently.

If you go to Wikipedia, you'll see four purported recipes for the fabled beverage. All include the processed coca leaves—which also can be a source of cocaine—but the company refuses to comment on whether coca leaves are still used to make its drinks. The Wikipedia recipes vary greatly, including everything from coriander and nutmeg to lime juice and lavender oils. Yet the actual recipe remains a secret to this day, and Coca-Cola remains ranked as the number six global brand in the world as of May 2011.

People are fascinated with secrets and mysteries. Whether we're talking about the secret ingredient in one of the most successful products in modern history, the mystery of life in other solar systems, or the search for the secret to a healthy and happy long life, it's human nature to seek to understand hidden truths that could benefit us in some way.

When it comes to the high-energy culture in business, the "secret sauce" is the *atmosphere*. As Einstein's quote indicates, you can't count it

... but does it ever count! In this chapter we capture the secret sauce of your organization ... or if there is a missing ingredient, we will bring it to light.

BREATHING IN THE ATMOSPHERE

Companies that have a strong channel for effective energy transfer are extraordinarily successful. This "channel" is the atmosphere within an organization, which differs from an organization's culture in a subtle but very important way. An organization's *culture* is the collection of norms that includes values, beliefs, decision-making style, and interpersonal interaction. It refers to physical elements within an organization that can be observed. The *atmosphere* of an organization is about the space between the bodies. It can't be observed, but it can be felt. The degree to which it's felt is directly proportional to the intensity of the resonating energy within the culture.

Think Apple. Apple's corporate culture has been described as "cult like" for its unique antiestablishment corporate style that transforms dress code, meeting protocol, flex hours, and even cafeteria dining to extraordinary degrees. But it's the atmosphere of innovation and creativity that includes operations excellence that drives the business to heights others envy and yearn to imitate. Until Steve Jobs stepped down as CEO a few months before his death in early October 2011, that energy started at the top with his overtly infectious spirit and cascaded down the ranks.

It is not the culture that drives economic value as much as it is the atmosphere. This may not be as counterintuitive as it seems. Think of the culture as the engine and the atmosphere as the fuel. Imagine starting a business on the basis of a relaxed dress code, generous employee perks, and an extremely comfortable office space. Sounds great, but without a viable business model headed by a talented, passionate, and energizing leader, it will fail quickly.

To be effective, to drive enormous economic value, your organization's atmosphere—your secret sauce—must be captured and clearly defined by you, the leader. You need to be the one to crack the code and demystify it for your team ... or you may need to determine the "missing ingredient" that will make your sauce special. Either way, you need to breathe in your atmosphere and dissect its components.

The unique truths of your culture, identified, clarified, and confirmed as accurate, are the only means to defining an atmosphere where energy can be transferred efficiently and effectively. This is the key to creating a strong channel that will allow your amplified energy to resonate throughout your company's culture. The secret revealed in this chapter is a secret Steve Jobs knew but no one is talking about.

THE ALLEN CURVE

One reason that the secret sauce remains elusive—and threatens to become more so—is life in the digital age as well as the global economy. Powerful communication is critical to organizational success, and yet it must take place across multiple time zones and great distances, more than ever before.

If you take a ride on the Tube in London, you'll hear repeated recorded announcements reminding you to "mind the gap" as you step across the space separating the platform from the train car. Yet "mind the gap" is also good advice as we think about how communication needs to transcend distance in the digital age.

One helpful concept here is the Allen curve. Years ago, MIT professor Thomas Allen performed a study in which he discovered that the frequency of communication between engineers decreased exponentially as the distance between them increased. He found that a distance of 50 meters or less was optimal.

Obviously, we can't pack whole organizations into 50 square meters. What to do? First, you need to take steps to ensure that all your organization's leaders understand your secret sauce and know how to share its power with their people. Second, you need to take steps to ensure that your communication culture is so strong that the Big Ideas behind your atmosphere can be transmitted through multiple people across a wide array of time zones and offices. Effective consulting expertise on strategic communication that drives economic value requires demonstrated real-life experience and a keen understanding of all the areas that are critical to a comprehensive communication strategy. You can't execute if you can't communicate. And you can't communicate if you don't understand the how, what, where, and when. For example, when we advise companies on how to assess the effectiveness of their communication strategy, we typically find a lack of understanding about the "degrees of separation" and the way communication decays through each medium, including:

- Face-to-face interaction—this is the *gold standard!*

- Face-to-group interaction (i.e., meetings).

- Videoconference.

- Personal phone call.

- Blast phone call or voice mail.

- Personal e-mail.

- Blast e-mail.

Margery Myers, an expert in communication strategy and former head of communications for Talbots and Dunkin Brands, and one of our premier consultants, always reminds our client companies of the importance of the gold standard. The more your communication has a face-to-face element or something close to it, the easier it is to ensure that the secret sauce of your atmosphere is conducted through the organization.

ENERGY TRANSFER AT GE

In my experience, energy transfer occurs most effectively when the leader is in close proximity to those she leads. Energized leaders who surround themselves with high-potential leaders can energize their followers through frequent and close interaction—a key to group cohesiveness. Jack Welch is one example. Over his 20-year tenure as CEO, his executive leadership team at General Electric was molded, shaped, and energized by his resonating energy. In turn, that energy flowed through the members of his leadership team to their direct reports, creating "the most talent-rich management bench in the world," according to top headhunters in the late 1990s. In spite of GE's enormous size, he created a small-company atmosphere that rewarded risk taking and performance in the spirit of *boundarylessness*, a word used to describe GE's secret sauce at that time. This term refers to the ability to cut through the bureaucracy that often bogs down large, complex organizations, preventing them from reaping the benefits of synergy.

Welch understood the impact his resonating energy had on the development of his high-potential leaders, which is why he personally participated hundreds of times in GE's world-class leadership development program in Crotonville, New York. His presence energized the emerging leaders in attendance and was a means of ensuring that his energy permeated the company. It was a brilliant way for Welch to transfer his energy through space and time and to energize the vast organization of General Electric. It was also a primary reason his personal truths created legendary shareholder value. During Welch's 20-year reign as CEO, he drove a staggering amount of economic value. According to www.valuebasedmanagement.net, GE's market value went from $12 billion in 1981 to approximately $280 billion in 2001. Controversial though his style may have been, Welch was true to his belief that there are no bounds to the human spirit. In another article, "How Jack Welch Runs GE," by John Byrnes, Welch stated his essential philosophy clearly and passionately: "The idea flow from the human spirit is absolutely unlimited. All you have to do is tap into that well . . . It's a belief that every person counts." Jack Welch's passion, born of his personal truths, is unambiguous, and it energized an entire company.

More remarkable and rare is how one leader can have such a profound impact on a company the size of General Electric. As we described with the Allen curve, there are only two possible ways the natural energy of one body (you, as a leader) can *greatly* amplify the energy of the people in and around your organization. One, you must be close enough to conduct the energy directly, just as a laptop computer must be within a small distance of a wireless signal. Or, two, as the distance from the leader increases, there must be some sort of channel that allows the energy to travel effectively from one body to all others. It is this medium, *the atmosphere in your organization*, through which energy is transferred from body to body, allowing the energy of one leader to be conducted through a large organization, just as electrical wiring passes energy through walls, floors, and ceilings. As in the case of GE, the energized culture is the means to real economic value—steep growth, market-share dominance, and impressive shareholder value.

PHASE 3. ALIGNMENT INTENSIFIES COMMITMENT

When you are able to crack the code by capturing the secret sauce of your atmosphere, you create a channel to spread your energy throughout the organization. The atmosphere is the energizing "oxygen" that allows people to operate at optimal levels of focus, self-motivation, and synchronized effort. There is great economic value when the organizational truths are clear and accurate and they align with the personal truths of the people in and around the organization.

In the last chapter, we talked about acknowledgment and accuracy. So now we move to the third A, which is alignment. Alignment creates deep commitment to the company and to the business strategy; it is a catalyst for self-motivation. Everyone in and around the organization is acting on a clear understanding of common truths that are important to each and to the collective whole. Everyone's actions are consistent with your own actions and expectations, regardless of whether you are present and watching or not.

If you correctly identify the truths that are the ingredients of your company's secret sauce, thus defining your unique atmosphere, you have created the means to produce enormous economic value.

Synchronizing the energy of all your company's resources with your own creates extraordinary power and gives your organization a distinct competitive advantage.

So let's talk about how to capture your secret sauce in a way that will effectively promote the transfer of powerful energy, giving your organization the opportunity to pull ahead of the pack. Now we have moved into the uppermost region of Quadrant III of our resonating energy continuum, as you can see in Figure 7.1.

When you crack the code as the leader, you create *predictability* and *capacity*. *Predictability* means that whenever the opportunity for energy transfer is present, it is almost guaranteed to occur. But if your organiza-

FIGURE 7.1 | THE ENERGY CONTINUUM

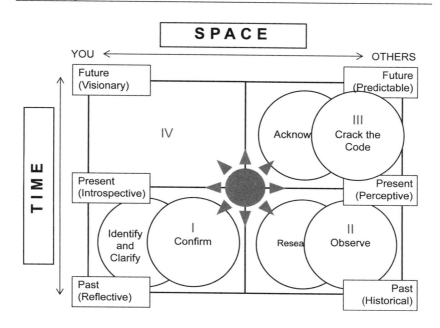

tion's atmosphere has a missing ingredient or the wrong recipe, the energy is dampened or even destructive. It can be like the symphony we spoke of early on, where one instrument out of tune or out of sync can diminish or destroy the pleasing effect of the whole. Clarity of the organization's truths, understood by all, allows energy to spread and employees to flourish.

Capacity means you have an atmosphere that is capable of handling any amount of energy you create through your words, actions, and behaviors. Even more, the atmosphere is capable of transferring the energy created by anyone else in and around your organization to all others. The system is *fully* capable of leveraging this power to an *unlimited* magnitude.

THE LAW OF ENERGY ATTRACTION

Legendary college basketball coach John Wooden was so confident that his organizational values, along with those of UCLA basketball and UCLA itself, were eminently powerful that he would not set up a meeting with a prospective high school recruit until and unless that player (or an associate) initiated the process by inquiring and showing interest. This recruiting philosophy was so far outside the norm that most coaches either never considered it or rejected it, preferring the traditional approach of scouting for initiating contact with top talent. Coach Wooden's approach was not a function of hubris—quite the contrary. He felt that the university's values were important, and he shared them as his own personal truths. He believed they had an attractive power that gave UCLA and him a competitive advantage. Further, he believed that unless these truths resonated with a recruit, compelling him to contact UCLA, "then perhaps it was best he attended another school."

Coach Wooden understood the tactic's risk and had the courage to remain steadfast in what he believed. Basically, he believed in what I call the *law of energy attraction*. When you create a high-energy culture, it's an incredibly attractive force. Every great performer wants to be a part of a winning team, whether in sports or in business. High-energy leaders attract high-energy contributors. It definitely worked for Coach Wooden. In 27 seasons as UCLA's head basketball coach, his records remain unmatched—316 wins to 68 losses, a .823 winning percentage, 4 undefeated seasons, 19 conference championships, and 10 NCAA national championships. He is often regarded as the best college basketball coach of all time. Of course, this level of success does not come without talent—personal talent and talented players. The list of talented players is long, but one who stands out is Lewis Alcindor, Jr., later known as Kareem Abdul-Jabbar.

Alcindor was one of the most highly recruited high school players in history. He could have attended any school in Division I to play basketball; many first-rate programs were close to his home in New York City. True to his philosophy, Coach Wooden did not initiate the conversation with Lewis or his family; they made first contact with Wooden. Upon reflection, Coach Wooden believes it was Lewis's parents who were compelled to start the conversation with UCLA because of four factors: clear evidence of equality, scholastic merit, credible and heartfelt testimonials from many influential sources such as Nobel laureate Dr. Ralph Bunche and baseball great Jackie Robinson, and Coach Wooden's reputed "color blindness." In *Wooden on Leadership*, Coach Wooden writes: "Good values are like a magnet, they attract good people." When Lewis came to

UCLA, the Bruins won three consecutive national championships, and their record was 88–2 over those three years.

Coach Wooden's personal truths aligned with his organization's truths. This alignment gave him the courage and the confidence to leverage the truths and drive value into his "business."

ALIGNMENT MEANS PUTTING THE PUZZLE TOGETHER

Begin by taking what you've learned and stringing the elements together in a meaningful way. You have likely already begun this process subconsciously. To do this deliberately we will now focus on the pieces individually. These are your findings from the previous chapters that are external to your own personal truths. Your own PTs are clear, present, and actionable now. Your focus here is on the truths you identified when you researched the legends, listened intently to the folklore, and observed the Alpha Dogs. It is what you learned when you queried the key players through dynamic inquiry. And, we'll do this from your perspective, because you are the leader.

Acknowledging the importance of the input from these employees, customers, vendors, and investors was an important step in the process because it demonstrated your belief in their value. It empowered them, just as Jack Welch empowered his emerging leaders with his presence in Crotonville. Your credibility undoubtedly increased as a result of your diligence to genuinely seek the input of your key players. However, you're the one who must now align what you have learned, because the power of the energy inside of *you* will be the guide as you determine what the organization's fundamental truths are. *Alignment is the confluence of analysis, contemplation, and "feel"* (see Figure 7.2). Your objective is to define the secret sauce that gives you and your organization a competitive advantage.

So what are the fundamental truths of your organization? Let's begin by aligning and clarifying what you have learned from doing the exercises in Chapters 4, 5, and 6. To do this, we will use a mind-mapping technique that will help you organize and think about the organizational truths you have gathered in a holistic and thought-provoking manner. This technique is not complicated, but it does require you to synthesize

FIGURE 7.2 | ALIGNMENT

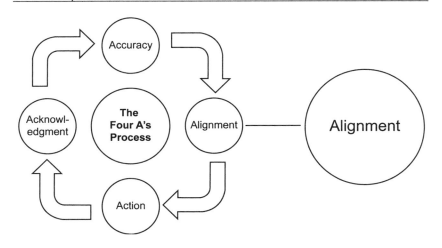

the basic set of core truths from a potentially lengthy list. Done correctly, it allows you to internalize what you have learned, process it, and then focus it through *your* personal lens. This activity can provide an epiphany of epic proportion about how you view your company. It will define the heart of your company, thereby enabling you to truly amplify its vibrating resonance through your leadership.

A *mind map* is a simple diagram used to represent words and ideas linked to and arranged around a central idea. It can be an effective tool to generate, visualize, structure, and clarify ideas and to organize information. The example that follows illustrates how, by carefully analyzing the expressed truths of various individuals within our organization, we were able to bring into focus the underlying truths. We were able to get beneath the tautology. The concept of "Walk the Talk" is consistent with the concept of "integrity," thereby supporting our definition of integrity as an organizational truth. Similarly, the concept of "Raise the Bar" is closely aligned with "driving results" and thus supports our definition of driving results as an organizational truth. It is important that you spend the time necessary to dig out these underlying "golden truths" for your own organization (see Figure 7.3).

The objective is to identify three to five words or phrases that define the atmosphere of your organization by assimilating, analyzing, and

FIGURE 7.3 | CORE TRUTHS

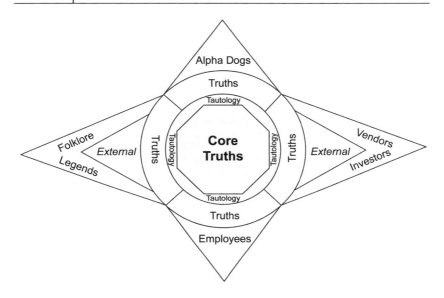

thinking about the information you've gathered. When you attempt to *crack the code,* it is important to seek the deeper meaning behind the words people have used. It's important that you, and you alone, are doing the thinking here. You have researched, observed, listened, and clarified what you heard. Putting all this information together is like assembling a puzzle whose image begins to emerge as the pieces fit together. That's your job now.

Which truths are most meaningful? Why these? The exercise at the end of the chapter—"The Story of the Secret Sauce"—will walk you through the process of figuring this out.

Don't overthink it! Let the truths emerge. As you contemplate the big picture and reflect on the fundamental truths of your organization, they will become clear. It's like an optical illusion: The harder you focus, the more elusive the image buried within becomes. My wife has a very effective tool for finding the "holes" in our Christmas tree light pattern, a trick she learned from her dad. She stands about 10 feet away from the tree and squints hard. When she does this, all she can discern is the pattern of lights outlining the tree. It becomes easy to see where there are too many lights or too few. Do the same here. Mentally take a step back from the information you've gathered about your organization's truths and squint. Suddenly, the fundamental truths that shape your own organization and form its secret sauce will become clear.

THE POWER OF WORDS

Language is important. Social resonance is enhanced when you choose the right words or phrases to represent your company's secret sauce. Conversely, resonance is unaltered or even diminished by the wrong words or phrases. A critical milestone during the creation of our Leadership Development Institute occurred when Holly had the epiphany leading to the final definition of our organization's atmosphere. It occurred as she was listening to our CEO address a group of bankers; his description of the organization's values struck Holly as so poignant, it had an emotional impact on her, prompting a revelation. His words were that powerful.

As I noted in an earlier chapter, the phrases we chose to represent our organization were *Walk the Talk, Raise the Bar,* and *Be One Team.* Yet these words did not elicit the reaction we were seeking. They were necessary but not sufficient. Consistent with our organization's truths, we needed to dive deeper, to reach the next level of understanding where our definition was so abundantly clear that when read by anyone associated with our company, inside or out, its words would evoke a reaction. For those who knew us, we wanted the reaction to be an affirmation—"Yes, that's exactly the culture I know." For those who did not know us, we wanted the reaction to be one of attraction *if* the words and phrases resonated with their own personal truths. If not, we wanted the reaction to actually repel them.

Why would a business want to repel a potential client or customer? There are many legitimate reasons. One great example comes from the early years of McDonald's. According to *Making History: A History of the United States Since 1865* by Carol Berkin et al., the McDonald brothers, Maurice and Richard, actually were doing quite well financially with a traditional drive-in restaurant model. As a carhop drive-in, a store could handle 125 cars at a time, and the menu was relatively broad, including ribs as well as barbecued pork and beef sandwiches in addition to traditional hamburgers.

Yet the brothers weren't happy with what their business was. It didn't resonate with their personal truths about who they were and what they wanted to be. They saw an opportunity to be more streamlined and efficient, and they envisioned their brand as a simple, clean restaurant that provided good value for families. However, this meant saying no to some easy money. By eliminating various revenue generators—jukeboxes, cigarette machines, pay phones, newsstands, and carhops—they were actively attempting to *discourage* teenagers from patronizing their business. In fact, they even determined that the carhops were unreliable employees and tended to attract leather-jacketed teenagers.

This line of thinking—later built upon when the business was taken over by Ray Kroc—may have seemed counterintuitive to pennywise restaurant owners of the 1950s. However, it's foundational to the fact that McDonald's is the fourth most recognized global brand as of May 2011.

Likewise, we decided to accept the fact that we might repel potential customers or employees. We discussed this and decided that the risk was minimal in comparison to the reward. It doesn't take a lot of reflection on the three fundamental truths in Figure 7.4 to understand how we came to this conclusion. Customers or potential employees who are repelled by these three truths are likely not the ones for us anyway. As Coach Wooden might say, perhaps it would be best if they went to the competition!

Our organizational truths emerged naturally and became a powerful economic driver for our company. We literally doubled the size of our business, gobbled up huge chunks of market share, and became more efficient, productive, and profitable than ever before in our history, all this during the most challenging economic times since the Great Depression, in a business segment—retail furniture—that was devastated by consumers' fear and limited discretionary income. Read the truths in Figure 7.4 and make note of how they make you feel.

How you choose to communicate your truths matters, and we'll cover this in the next chapter, as we turn our focus to *action* (the fourth A).

Suffice to say that right now you *must* be careful to choose "actionable" words and phrases to define your organization's atmosphere. Just as

FIGURE 7.4 | THE THREE FUNDAMENTAL TRUTHS

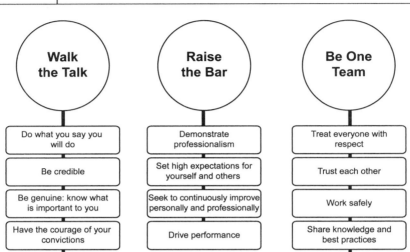

with your personal truths, your organization's truths must prompt action in order to transmit energy at the same frequency as that of all those associated with your organization.

When leaders define, clarify, and act in lockstep with their own personal truths, the energy inside them is enhanced, and the potential for this powerful energy to resonate with others is present.

It is the same with the organization's truths. When the people in and around your organization are clear on these truths, and these truths are defined in a way that touches their hearts and minds, then the channel through which the energy can travel has been established. You've created *predictability*.

WHAT IF YOU BUILT IT AND THEY DIDN'T COME?

Remember the baseball movie *Field of Dreams*? In it, Kevin Costner plays an Iowa farmer who hears a voice saying, "If you build it, they will come." He has a vision of a baseball field amid his profit-yielding cornstalks. He listens to the voices, and against all odds, people flock to his door to play catch on his baseball field by the end of his movie, saving him and his family from financial ruin.

Real life doesn't always go this way, however. In fact, one recent business book is entitled *So You Built It and They Didn't Come. Now What?* The book addresses what an entrepreneur should do after investing considerable money into a business, only to find that customers don't arrive in droves as they did at the Field of Dreams.

A parallel emerges here. What if you're reading this from the perspective of someone whose organization is in dire need of an energy transfusion? In that case, you aren't looking to capture the secret sauce. You don't *have* one. Your goal is to determine the missing ingredient. Regardless, the process is similar. Close inspection of your personal truths as well as examination of legends and folklore in comparison to the very real perceptions of Alpha Dogs, employees, vendors, and investors should reveal some inconsistencies that you need to address. What missing ingredient could be added to correct your misaligned atmosphere? The processes I've described here will help uncover it.

In the next chapter, we will explore how you can create capacity so your company's atmosphere can handle unlimited energy. You have begun to create a distinct competitive advantage with increasing economic value. Now your job is to leverage this value and turn it into tangible results.

The Story of Your Secret Sauce

Storytelling is a powerful communication tool and one we will explore in detail in Chapter 9, when we describe fully and thoroughly explore the concept of the Bates Story Structure. As a brief preview, here are the key elements:

1. *The setup.* This is the who, what, when, and where of the story, told succinctly.

2. *The buildup.* This describes a conflict, a problem, a challenge that must be faced.

3. *The scene.* This is a "snapshot in time" where we drill into a specific turn of events, such as a critical conversation or sequence of events.

4. *The resolution.* We need to see the outcome of the story: How was the problem or challenge resolved?

5. *The lesson.* What did you learn from this experience? How did it change you?

6. *The audience theme.* How does what you learned relate to what you want the listener of the story to take away from it?

Storytelling is also an excellent tool to help give us clues to elements of our secret sauce. So, in this exercise we ask you to think of a story that best represents your organization's secret sauce . . . or one that will help you determine the missing ingredient. Here are the steps:

1. *Close your eyes and think of a specific story that captures the atmosphere of your organization today.* It could be anything: a success,

a challenge, a problem, an obstacle. The key is to pick a story that really captures what it feels like to work at your company. Be specific: Use the Bates Story Structure to give us a setup, buildup, scene, and resolution.

2. *Now think about the* lesson *of this story.* Reflect on your internal and external search for truth about your organization. What insight does this story give us about your culture? What is the story telling us?

3. *If the insight is* positive, *use it to craft a short statement defining the special sauce of your organization.*

4. *If the insight is* negative, *use it to craft a short statement defining the missing ingredient in your organization's special sauce.*

5. *If the insight is mixed, use it to craft a short statement about how you might tweak the recipe to give the sauce the magic it needs.*

Do not get too concerned if your story is not following all six key elements correctly. We will focus more on this later. The insight the story provides is the goal right now.

Promote Your Resonating Culture

I sound my barbaric YAWP over the roofs of the world!
—WALT WHITMAN, AMERICAN POET,
ESSAYIST, AND JOURNALIST

Communication is the great unaddressed issue in most organizations today. As a leadership competency, communication is more powerful than all other competencies combined. I say this with great conviction and confidence. As a business leader, you may be thinking "So what will the steps I've taken to this point in the process do for my business?" And the answer is . . . nothing! Not yet at least. You can't answer *any* "so-what?" questions without powerful leadership communication skills. They not only address the "so whats?" They translate all the hard work you've done up until this point into real, tangible economic value. These "so-what?" questions include:

- *So what* if you have an atmosphere that allows for the transfer of powerful energy?

- *So what* if you are a leader who is clear on your personal truths and you courageously commit to acting consistent with them?

- *So what* if you are clear now on your organization's truths?

- *So what* if they align with your own?

All the great work we've done so far is for naught if you, as a leader, cannot communicate effectively.

I would be remiss if I didn't back up my bold statement by defining communication in the context of leadership. Bates Communications defines leadership communication as "the effective use of the collective means a leader has available to connect with another human being or group of human beings to promote understanding and to marshal action."

Note that leadership communication, as we define it, is both visual and nonvisual. This means that effective communication is as much a function of what your audience *observes* (visual) as what it *hears and feels* (nonvisual). Ultimately, you want to marshal the action of your audience with your communication so the organization moves in its intended strategic direction. It's not just nice to do. These actions drive performance, move your business forward, and create tangible economic value.

The sole measure of your effectiveness as a communicator in business is how well your message, your timing of delivery, your style of delivery, and your behaviors marshal actions that drive tangible business results.

A MARRIAGE OF ART AND SCIENCE

Communication as defined here is a marriage of art and science. The best business leaders know the art *and* the science of communicating. Alan Mulally, CEO of Ford, is a great example. As I mentioned in the legends and folklore chapter, he is one of the hottest CEOs on the planet. He turned around the floundering Ford Motor Company and led the Big Three automaker out of the recession faster, better, and more successfully than either GM or Chrysler did. Under his leadership, Ford was able to avoid government bailout capital, trim its portfolio of brands to refocus on the core Ford brands, and retool and reengineer production to manufacture its Eco-Boost high-performance engines. Mulally is a skillful communicator. He marshaled the actions of his employees with his open communication style. In just five years, Ford turned from near insolvency to a profit of $6.6 billion in 2010.

Mulally is an engineer, and his communication style by nature is technical; yet he has mastered speaking to his audience's minds *and* hearts using the art of storytelling. In fact, Mulally was a student of persuasive communication going back to his childhood, when he sat up front in church because he admired his minister and sought to understand what made him such an effective speaker.

At the Detroit Athletic Club, where he accepted the Automotive Executive of the Year award, he told the story of his first day at Ford. He was walking through the executive parking lot and noticed there were only Jaguars, Land Rovers, and Aston Martins in the parking spots. All foreign brands owned by Ford, but no Fords were anywhere to be seen. "The case seemed clear," he said to the audience. "If Ford brass won't drive Fords, who will?" This endeared him to the audience, which was located in the heart and soul of America's auto manufacturing industry within an institution whose founding members include automotive pioneers. Mulally gets the power of communication and uses his competence to drive business results.

To connect what is inside us to what is inside others, we are limited to one means—the art of communication.

We now move into the final quadrant, Quadrant IV, of our energy continuum (see Figure 8.1).

FIGURE 8.1 | THE ENERGY CONTINUUM

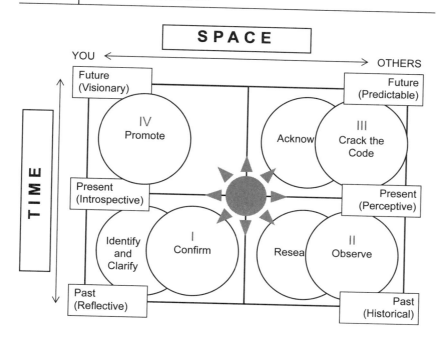

THE STAGGERING COST OF POOR LEADERSHIP COMMUNICATION

Going back to my days at Raymour & Flanigan, Holly, Phil, and I were in year three of our Leadership Development Institute. By this time, we had fine-tuned the programs. The institute was recognized as a success within our company and around the retail industry. By 2009, our company had responded to CEO Neil Goldberg's fateful announcement at that Connecticut bar. After he told us "we're going in," he did Michael Jordan proud by elevating our game as he always had. The upshot was that we had targeted and penetrated the largest and most discerning retail market in the world. We were grabbing market share in enormous chunks. The economy was at the height of the recession, and furniture sales throughout the industry were declining steadily. The competition, both large and small, was failing—either going out of business or scaling back to survive. Yet the markets we were in still represented $10 billion in furniture sales annually. During the first three years of our development initiatives, our company jumped from 5 percent to 10 percent of the total share.

Over this three-year period we created four custom curricula intended to build our leaders organically. We had put nearly 500 of our leaders and emerging leaders through these programs beginning with the executive team and working downward. By studying the results gleaned from our rigorous assessments and obtained through our interactive curricula, and simply by interacting with the leaders in and out of the classroom while they were captive on our campus, we got to know all of them very well.

It was during a capstone exercise where we caught our first glimpse of something that was missing. This exercise was designed to focus our top leaders on an innovative business idea that they would choose to develop and present to "the board." For this portion, in other words, one of the owners of the company typically would participate in the exercise by evaluating the ideas as well as the group's presentation skills. The primary purpose of the exercise was to help leaders collaborate cross-functionally using all that they learned about themselves, including:

- ▶ Their style of leading

- ▶ Their emotional intelligence

- ▶ Their ability to listen and build influence

- ▶ Their ability to participate in a team environment

A key attribute for our best leaders was to lead teams to become high performing. We defined high-performing teams using a variation of the definition coined by John Katzenbach and Doug Smith in their book *The Wisdom of Teams*. In our metric-focused environment, a high-performing team was one that consistently outperformed all similar teams in reasonable categories of measurement over an extended period.

The residual benefits we expected from this capstone exercise were many. We anticipated that we'd have a better understanding of the demands and challenges in other operating areas of the business as well as in other geographies. We thought we'd also have a clearer sense of how the service functions at our corporate campus could and should help at the operating level. It was a fascinating exercise with ideas and discussion that proved invaluable to our organization. However, one critical finding that emerged somewhat unexpectedly proved most valuable.

We began to observe that many of the best leaders, who were extremely knowledgeable and capable within their area of influence, were not influencing the decisions of their assigned group in a way that maximized the outcome. During the group interaction process, we facilitators were merely observers, and so we had occasion to see how each participant was interacting. Our idea was to quietly capture some observations about each that we would review with the participants in a one-on-one session later.

When we compared our notes, we found that each of us had observed a similar phenomenon. Many of our best leaders were not expressing their thoughts in a way that caught the group's attention and influenced the ultimate decision. They either were reluctant to say what they were thinking or feeling or were simply too comfortable, allowing the one or two dominant people in the group to take the process in a direction they felt was best. When Holly, Phil, and I found that we each had witnessed similar behaviors in our groups, we began to discuss the implications. Knowing the leaders as we did, we were immediately struck by the opportunity cost of a quiet or ineffective leader in a group setting to our business, let alone to the outcome of the exercise.

ENSURING YOU'LL BE HEARD

I remember one particularly distressing situation. A store manager in Yonkers, one of the areas in metropolitan New York City that we had recently penetrated, was frustrated by the queue that was created at the customer service desk area during high-traffic periods. Our standard procedure was for the sales associate to walk the customer over to the service desk once the customer had made the "buy" decision. Service desk associates would then create the final sales order paperwork and obtain the customer's signature, thus consummating the sale. During high-traffic periods, the line at the desk would grow, and so would the risk of "buyer's remorse" if customers were stuck in line. They were anxious to move on now that they had made their decision, particularly in a market where every consumer is used to a fast pace and instant gratification.

This store manager strongly believed that a sales associate equipped with a handheld device could expedite the process. He was well aware that the potential value for the company would be enormous because he knew the metrics supporting lost sales due to waiting. Scanned bar codes would electronically convert sales orders, thereby minimizing the time at the customer service desk. A very good idea from every business analysis perspective. He even said to me, "We spend *millions* on marketing to consumers who may or may not come and shop at our stores while we are losing customers who have *already decided* to buy at our store." Wow! That was like a brick to the side of my head. Yet in his group, the idea never made it past casual consideration during the early part of the brainstorming process. Why? A very dominant leader in the group of communicators felt his idea was more innovative and appropriate to pursue.

Holly and Phil had witnessed similar situations in their groups. Like me, they knew the leaders well and were disappointed that many of the best were not being more influential, and in some cases, were not even being heard. We started to estimate the economic value of this lost opportunity. It made my head spin. Needless to say, it represented perhaps tens of millions of bottom-line dollars. We concluded that a communication problem was at the heart of the issue and that "fixing" the communication problem had a real and tangible return on investment (ROI). Definitively stated, the problem was this: *Leaders who cannot or who choose not to express themselves in a way that ensures they are heard and their important input is considered are an opportunity cost to our business.*

We embarked on a plan to incorporate leadership communication into our highest-level leadership development program. After significant evaluation of potential resources that could help us with our leaders' communication challenges, we found Bates Communications to be the one resource that connects effective communication to strategy, execution, and, ultimately, to tangible economic value. Then a very curious thing happened. I was so compelled by what Suzanne Bates and her talented team do, I joined the company. Unfortunately, this decision meant that I could not participate in the ongoing development of the many talented and dedicated leaders at Raymour & Flanigan, but it opened up the universe of opportunities for leaders just like them everywhere who can become best-in-class by focusing on the core leadership competency of powerful communication. Now, I'm pursuing my passion to help these leaders become the very best they can be. Companies that recognize the importance of leaders who communicate effectively, and that act on that recognition, create an enormous competitive advantage for their business. One of Apple's distinctive competencies is the company's ability to prompt creativity and encourage it from everyone. In fact, not only is creativity encouraged at Apple, but it's required. Apple's atmosphere catalyzes creativity, and the leadership is energized to marshal action from employees, vendors, indeed all of its stakeholders, giving the company an enormous advantage.

What thinking does your atmosphere catalyze with regard to communication? Does your atmosphere welcome input and ensure that all good ideas are heard? You should have a very good answer to this question given your work from Chapter 7. Now, armed with this understanding, you can use the power of *your* communication to leverage the channel that is your company's atmosphere. And it is powerful.

RED LIGHT, GREEN LIGHT

Back to Mulally. Prior to his arrival, the executive team at Ford would develop a business plan and meet two or three times a year to revisit it. Mulally brought the review of plans to weekly meetings and used a process he had created over the years to facilitate the review. Given that Ford is the seventh largest corporation in the United States and seventeenth largest in the world, you can imagine how much data the company leaders have to process. In fact, most large companies don't do so every month, let alone every Thursday morning.

If you're a member of the Ford leadership team, you need a system to get through everything in a 2½-hour meeting. In addition to knowing your data, you have to color-code progress in each area on a chart for all to see. If you're off target in readying for a launch, you would use yellow or red for coding, depending on how far off you are. If all is well, you use green . . . and the team knows immediately not to linger on it because all systems are go. So how was the new process accepted? Here's what happened, as Mulally explained in a videotaped interview with the *Washington Post*:

"This is a very interesting thing. When we started this process, we had gone a couple of weeks, and I just stopped the meeting because all of the metrics were green and the year before we had lost over $14 billion. And so I said in my nicest way, 'Is there *anything* that's not going well here, given that we lost $14 billion? So we had a conversation about that because it had to be okay for you to color your area of responsibility—not yourself—a yellow or a red.

"I'll never forget that maybe it was the next week where Mark Fields, who was leading the Americas, had a launch of the new Edge. They had an issue with a hinge on the back door that wasn't exactly right. We would need to work with the suppliers to get that fixed. So up comes this chart, and it was delaying production because of the launch. And he had colored it a bright red.

"The room got silent. How would the new CEO respond to this harbinger of bad news? Here was a red. Was a hook going to come out? Was Mark going to disappear? And I started to clap. I said, 'This is tremendous visibility, Mark, and what can we all do to help you?' Within

30 seconds, the manufacturing engineer had an idea; the procurement leader had an idea from a supplier he was working with.

"Next week, the red turned to a yellow. The week after that, the yellow turned to a green. But the neatest thing was that following week, all of the charts had become a rainbow because it was okay and *expected* that each of us share where we *really* are. It has to be a safe environment, but also you can imagine the accountability that goes with that. What I have found is that the more you create an environment where everybody knows everything, then the faster you're going to be able to bring help to bear.

"So it's not a punitive thing: It's not that *you're* red. It's your area of responsibility, and you're sharing with us and the team that you need help.

"It was just a different culture that we were going to bring in. With all the vehicles that we're working on at the same time, everybody really embraced this system because then they were going to get the help and visibility that they never would've gotten if they didn't bring the issue forward."

I would disagree with Mr. Mulally on one word only—*culture*. He was bringing in a different *atmosphere*, not culture. The Ford culture was ingrained long before him, beginning with Henry Ford himself. The point is that Alan Mulally is a leader who understands the power of aligning his personal truths with his actions, thus creating an atmosphere that amplifies energy at the same frequency in everyone around. His leadership team was energized to bring problems forward and use the collective intellect, experience, and capability of all the resources Ford had at its beck and call to make a difference. And imagine if everyone on the leadership team was able to create a similar process within his organization? This energy, channeled through the atmosphere of Ford, was primal in turning the business around. And it all began with one energized leader, Alan Mulally, and his understanding of and commitment to communication.

A recent Towers Watson study on ROI supported the importance of communication. The study found that "companies [with leaders] that are highly effective communicators had 47 percent higher total returns to shareholders over the last five years compared to firms that are the least effective communicators." At Bates, we are often asked about how communication creates economic value. The answer: by marshaling the

FIGURE 8.2 | ACTION

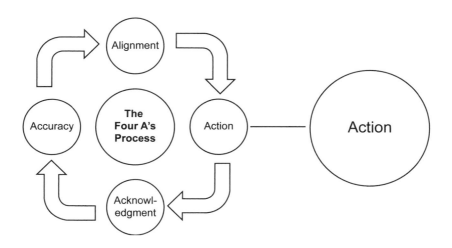

action of anyone and everyone within the atmosphere toward an end state that you envision (see Figure 8.2).

PHASE 4. ACTION THAT CREATES EXECUTION

It is the collective action of everyone you influence that determines the results you drive as a leader.

This is true for you, Steve Jobs, A. G. Lafley, Kathy Ireland, Vince Lombardi, Dr. Phil Martin, and me. It's true for any leader over the history of time, and it's true for any leaders going forward.

FROM WHITE BELT TO MASTER

Let's dissect this and study it more deeply. Fundamentally, in a business, communication is the means by which two or more parties connect. Think of the art of communication in this setting as you would the levels of expertise in a form of martial arts. My wife is a second-degree black belt in tae kwon do. Although I'm a former college football player, I'm very careful *never* to upset her. When she was just beginning to learn the art, she was taught the most basic elements that are essential to master first, such as how to make a fist, how to punch and kick properly, and how to protect herself from injury. Mastering these fundamentals as a white belt was the goal of this first belt level. Of course, before even beginning to learn these fundamentals, there was a level of commitment as well as a set of basic physical and mental requirements that she must demonstrate as the price of entry. For instance, she had to be physically capable of handling the rigors of the art, and she had to commit herself to practicing, attending the classes, and showing up ready to learn.

Similarly, communication skills at the leadership level involve specific capabilities at each level of expertise. At the lowest level are skills and behaviors that are the price of entry for leaders. For instance, leaders must have excellent written and oral skills. I am always taken aback by the way some leaders choose to express themselves in writing or orally. It can devalue your leadership brand with just a few carelessly written or ill-spoken words to anyone on the receiving end. Poor written and oral communication skills will definitely keep you out of the top echelon of the best leaders. So if that is where you strive to reside, then start here. Isn't it interesting how often we see the imperative "excellent written and verbal skills" in recruiting ads for executive-level candidates?

Assuming you have these entry-level skills, then the white-belt level of leadership communication would be learning basic presentation skills: understanding the members of your audience, connecting with what's on their mind, and identifying your Big Idea. Creating a presentation that engages the audience, hitting the key points accurately and succinctly, and delivering it consistent with your personal leadership brand is a "first-level" skill for leaders intent on mastering communication. It may surprise you to learn that presentation skills for a leader are in the yellow-belt level of leadership communication. Mastering these skills takes practice, and when mastered, you are still only at yellow-belt status. If we continue the analogy, then the various levels would look something like what you see in Table 8.1.

Craig Bentley, one of our premiere executive coaches, would ask, *"How do you hard-wire your communication skills to enhance your bottom-line results?"* This is your goal. You want to leverage all the work you have done to this point and begin to develop a 30-second message that speaks

TABLE 8.1 | TAE KWON DO AND LEADERSHIP COMMUNICATION

	Tae Kwon Do	Leadership Communication
Price of entry	Physical fitness and personal commitment	Excellent written and oral skills
White	Basics of punching and kicking; basic patterns	Basic presentation skills
Yellow	More basic patterns; practice form and technique	Advanced presentation skills and executive presence
Green	Performing; more advanced punches and kicking; advanced patterns	Projecting authenticity and passion
Blue	Visualizing applications of patterns and techniques; weapons	Winning trust, gaining buy-in, and influencing
Red	Perfecting techniques; applying them in competition; teaching	Storytelling to engage your audience's hearts and minds, prompting self-motivation
Black	New beginning; learning, mastering, teaching	Marshaling action, aligning all stakeholders, energizing everyone
Master	Tenth degree	Steve Jobs = Blowing away the competition!

to the hearts and minds of your audience and catalyzes action from all the important stakeholders. Let's start by taking your epiphany from Chapter 7.

We will begin to establish a message that is powerful by tying your personal truths to the organizational truths. This is how you get to "green belt." The truths—your personal truths—that you have recommitted to are powerful. What you have learned about your organization is also powerful. To leverage the combined power of both, and to use the power of communication to send your amplifying energy out over the channel that is your organization's atmosphere, you must convey a clear, compelling message that resonates with everyone who can bring the desired end state to reality. This cascading energy will in turn energize everyone in and around your organization. When you get it right, you will have created the capacity by which unlimited energy can and will be carried to everyone in and around your company (see Figure 8.3).

FIGURE 8.3 | PERSONAL TRUTHS AND ATMOSPHERE

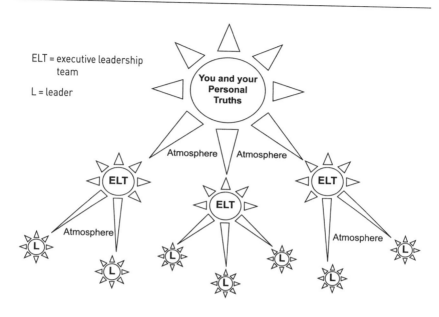

ELT = executive leadership team

L = leader

You and your Personal Truths

Atmosphere

Atmosphere

ELT

ELT

ELT

Atmosphere

Atmosphere

Atmosphere

L

L

L

L

L

L

CELEBRATING THE WINS

At Raymour & Flanigan, our CEO, Neil Goldberg, used the phrase "enhance the customer's shopping experience" often, well before we embarked on the yearlong exercise to clarify our organization's values. It was a strong message. Generally, everyone who heard it understood it. When Neil spoke these words, he was authentic and passionate. Yet he was only at green-belt level. The message wasn't reaching the hearts of the audience. It lacked the ability to amplify energy within the listeners.

Then we defined the organization truths as "Walk the Talk," "Raise the Bar," and "Be One Team." When we tied these truths to "enhance the customer's shopping experience," something special happened. Suddenly, the expanded message, spoken eloquently and passionately by Neil, reached the hearts as well as the minds of the audience. With the message described in this manner, employees were proud to be part of that one team. They knew Neil's message truly described who we were, and they used it to create their own messages. They began to get real and answer the question, "How will this team that I lead contribute to enhancing the customer shopping experience?"

Neil would expertly fashion the message to reach the hearts of other stakeholders. I remember a bankers' meeting I attended where he repurposed the words in a way that moved even the most conservative minded in the group. One of them came up to me after the meeting and said, "I've been through hundreds of these types of meetings, and never have I felt moved the way I was today."

We captured Neil on video and played it at internal meetings. When we celebrated our champions, we held them up as symbolic of these truths. When we recognized the best leaders in our company, we shared stories of how each of them *lived* these truths and acted on them in ways that truly enhanced our customers' shopping experiences. We put the message on banners so our customers could see it. Even more important, we wanted them to *feel* the message so compellingly that when they read it, they would nod and say, "Yes, *that* describes this remarkable company!" The message became powerful. So powerful was it in its simplicity and profundity that we put it on mugs and plaques and in our e-mail signatures. It was everywhere! It drew us together. At the same time, it energized everyone in and around our organization, driving us to act and propelling us forward.

Our sense of mission and purpose sustained us. Whether on a playing field or in the corporate field, great leaders always know that there is a tension between celebrating your wins and resting on your laurels. There were always more ways to enhance the customer's shopping experience, especially as we faced different competitors, macroeconomic challenges, and new markets. Our CEO's combination of energy and humility helped us strike just the right balance of these two traits. We had made mistakes along the way and knew that there were always new ones that could be made, just as there was always an opportunity for greater success. Spurred on by great leadership, we just kept fighting the good fight.

Think of your communication as though you were Martin Luther King, Jr., speaking into a microphone on the steps of the Lincoln Memorial, sending out a message that resonated with a nation. When you have mastered the art of communication, it is powerful, and it triggers a cascading effect. You get employees buzzing about why "it's good" for them personally. By reaching them at the level of their own personal truths, you stimulate their energy and gain their commitment. By reaching their hearts, you flip the switch of their self-motivation and focus their minds on the actions that are important to driving value. You get them working together in the spirit of shared purpose and camaraderie. You reduce the fear and negative assumptions that come from lack of clarity. Nothing derails morale and diminishes energy like distrust. When your communication is consistent and clear, you create trust and employee engagement.

Back in Chapter 1, I talked about the September 2010 Gallup research on employee engagement. As you recall, "engaged" organizations have 3.9 times the earnings-per-share growth rate compared with that of organizations with lower engagement in their same industry. World-class organizations have a roughly 10-to-1 ratio of engaged to disengaged employees, while average organizations have a ratio of about 2 to 1. Disengaged employees cost U.S. companies roughly $800 billion in productivity annually. Figure 8.4 can help you visualize it.

FIGURE 8.4 | RATIO OF ENGAGED TO DISENGAGED EMPLOYEES IN WORLD-CLASS AND AVERAGE COMPANIES

World-Class Companies:
Ratio of Engaged to Disengaged Employees

Average Companies:
Ratio of Engaged to Disengaged Employees

Bottom line—and I do mean quite literally the bottom line—it's your ability to communicate that has the greatest impact on engagement. In the organizational symphony, your voice is a powerful instrument that can inspire energy and emotion in your listeners. Communicate meaning, not just information, and see what power your words truly have to create the economic results you seek.

Business can be the means to exercise what is most important—to you and to those you lead. The economic results are your scorecard. The real value comes from the impact you have on the world, not so much the business. Steve Jobs said, "I want to make a ding in the universe." Vince Lombardi said, "We are going to relentlessly chase perfection . . . because in the process we will catch excellence."

What do you say?

Crafting an Energizing Message

Now it's time to think about how you can promote your resonating culture with your important audience. Your goal is to tie together the truths that you've gleaned from all sources and then craft a message that will inspire your listeners.

1. Think about your most important audiences: employees, customers, vendors, investors. Which of the audiences is in the greatest need of a transfusion of resonating energy?

   _____

   _____

2. Once you've identified that audience, write down the top three needs or questions or concerns of the toughest or most skeptical members of that group.

   _____

   _____

   _____

3. Craft a short speech to that audience. It doesn't have to be long—maybe six to eight sentences. It should include:

   ▸ An acknowledgment of a key concern, issue, fear, or question that this group legitimately feels.
   ▸ Your core truth as informed by your personal truths and all that you learned from your study of legends and folklore as well as from internal and external stakeholders.

▸ How your core truth connects to or how this truth motivates you to address the concern, issue, fear, or question that you identified.

_____

_____

_____

_____

_____

_____

4 . Once you've completed refining this statement, reflect on it. What impact would this statement have on your audience? When you've crafted your statement properly, your audience feels what you feel. Have you given your audience something to rally around, much as Alan Mulally has done with his use of legends as well as with empowering people through communication?

_____

_____

_____

_____

_____

_____

Create the Rally Cry

At an interview with a reporter during his first year as the new CEO of Ford, Alan Mulally was asked, "So how do you intend to fix Ford?" It would've been possible for an economics student to write a dissertation on this topic. What a complicated challenge, turning around the Ford Motor Company! You could write whole chapters on financing, marketing, manufacturing, and communications. The most mind-numbing PowerPoint slide in the history of visuals would not be able to capture the countless strategic and tactical steps that would be necessary to turn around a company that was losing billions of dollars annually.

So how did Mulally respond? He got up and went over to a cabinet in his office. He pulled out a plastic pen and a laminated 2" × 3" card. He handed both to the reporter and enthusiastically proclaimed, "*This* is how."

The pen had the Ford logo on it.

The card read "One Ford. One Team. One Plan. One Goal."

Simple. Yet very powerful. And as it turns out, very effective because it helped rally everyone in and around Ford to action. This simple and powerful message summed up a business strategy for a vast, far-reaching, and complex corporation in a way that energized the receivers and gave them a feeling of confidence that Mulally was bringing his vision to reality.

SIMPLE IS HARD

Simple is hard. That's the great irony of powerful leadership communication. The most powerful messages are the simplest . . . and the most difficult to construct. A powerful message pulls people in. When on point, the message speaks to their emotions. The best messages amplify energy within the receiver and prompt action. Leveraging the power of words does not mean taking a shotgun approach to blast out a large amount of ammunition, hoping one or two shots hit the target. It's more like being a sniper. You want to fire one bullet that hits the target precisely.

Too often, leaders get lost in language. Good leaders know their business and are passionate about their goals and vision, and so they are often quick to launch into a rapid-fire outburst of words to explain what is in their heads and hearts. They are teeming with energy; they just don't know how to focus it like a laser. Meanwhile, listeners become glassy eyed quicker than you can imagine. Their impatience turns to disengagement. Why? They are less concerned about what is in *your* head and heart and more concerned about what is in their own. It's human nature.

Your goal is to construct a simple message that speaks
to the heart of the recipient.

You can't do this if your message is packed with words, concepts, and details that overwhelm the mind and numb the emotions of the recipient. In today's digital age, people don't have time for elaborate explanations. We want something as bold and simple as "Buy an iPod and put your entire record collection in your pocket."

Here's a quote that's often attributed to Mark Twain: "I have made this letter longer than usual, only because I have not had time to make it shorter." In reality, it may actually have been the words of seventeenth-century French mathematician and philosopher Blaise Pascal. Regardless, the point is that it takes time and effort to be succinct.

Your message must be simple. It needs to answer the question, "So what is different about your company [or division, business unit, department, product, etc.]?" Your message also has to answer this question in the receiver's mind by tying the strategic heartbeat of your company to her own heartbeat. Your powerful message will marshal action from those who hear or read it, prompting them to act to drive the business forward. And this goes for people outside the company as well as inside.

Mulally's index card message is a good example: "One Ford. One Team. One Plan. One Goal." That's not just a message; it's a *Rally Cry.* Here are some others:

"Every day you get our best." Wegmans

"The happiest place on earth." Disneyland

"Whole Foods, Whole People, Whole Planet." Whole Foods

"Think Different." Apple

"There's always room for Jell-O." Jell-O

"Just Do It." Nike

There is a great deal of power packed into these little phrases—and many are more clever than you might think at first glance. For instance, Apple's "Think Different" telegraphs the idea that the company is defining itself as an alternative to IBM, whose motto was "Think." The Jell-O Rally Cry sounds like child's play, but it actually has a double meaning. To the average consumer, it captures the idea that Jell-O is a light dessert that you'll have room for after any meal . . . and yet it also was devised as a direct message to supermarkets: There's always room to fit those little boxes of Jell-O into whatever shelf space you have available. The phrase served Kraft as a powerful merchandising tool. But what do the most powerful messages do to serve their companies? Whenever I hear or read "Just Do It," my competitive nature is energized. As a former athlete, I find that the phrase conjures up the powerful emotions that I felt when competing. Somehow, my mind makes the transition to Nike apparel, and I am compelled to consider the company's merchandise for whatever I may be doing in the realm of exercise and sports. At the very least, I associate the brand with my own desire to win. Those three simple words speak to my emotions. They penetrate my heart and soul and serve to associate what's inside me with the essence of the Nike brand.

THE RALLY CRY

These simple Rally Cries capture the heartbeats of their companies while serving as cries for everyone who hears or reads them. Now step back and reflect. Your company's secret sauce is special. To be similarly powerful, your Rally Cry *must* capture the special nature of your secret ingredient.

> *Your Rally Cry is the vehicle that transports the energy inside of you outward into the atmosphere of your organization and beyond, where it cascades throughout and connects with everyone.*

In this chapter you will complete the steps necessary to fill the space in the energy continuum in Figure 9.1. In completing these steps you will be helped to craft your simple, powerful Rally Cry. Once it is crafted, you will learn how to deliver it powerfully.

FIGURE 9.1 | THE ENERGY CONTINUUM

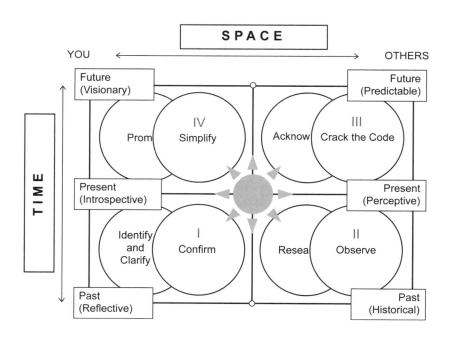

THE THREE RULES OF THE RALLY CRY

There are three rules that are essential and must be followed when crafting a simple, powerful Rally Cry:

Rule #1. It must be your own. Your Rally Cry has to be genuine. It must come from *your* heart and soul, and when people hear it, they must feel like it's coming from a real person.

Rule #2. It must be laser accurate. Your Rally Cry needs to ring true in the ears of the vast majority of your employees, customers, vendors, and investors.

Rule #3. It must answer the question, "What is different *about your company?"* Your Rally Cry has to speak to the single most defining and differentiating truth about your company that sets it apart. It must tie directly to the strategic heartbeat of your company. This is key.

Review the general pitch you constructed in the exercise from Chapter 8. If you have followed the process carefully, then this narrative should be filled with a thoughtful interpretation of what your company is all about and what matters to you as the leader. It should connect with employees, customers, and vendors. It is the raw material for the succinct, powerful Rally Cry you will now construct that will serve to energize all your important audiences. It will prompt action because it will speak to the hearts and minds of all your important audiences. Our goal now is to make your narrative pithy and juice it up! We want high-octane fuel to fire everyone's engine.

Make no mistake. This is not a gimmick, nor is it primarily a marketing or PR tool—although when it's right, it has great value for both those purposes. This is a communication tool first, and a very powerful one because it is charged with the energy of your personal truths. It is Neil Goldberg's "Enhance the customer's shopping experience." This is the core message that everything else you will communicate builds on. It is foundational, but it is also fundamental. Going forward, as you repeat your authentic, passionate, audience-focused communication, this simple Rally Cry will serve to represent all of what you say, believe, and do. It will remind everyone of the purpose and core truth of the company as embodied by you, the leader.

"Think Different" represents Apple's culture, a cult of creativity and innovation. Those two simple words also represent Steve Jobs and everything he believed. They helped to make Apple one of the most powerful forces in technology and one of the most successful and respected companies in business today. The people who matter most are moved to action by Mr. Jobs's enduring Rally Cry.

Your Rally Cry should evoke a positive buzz about:

▸ Where you are going

▸ Why you are going there

▸ Why it truly benefits everyone around you to participate

Three Perspectives on Your Rally Cry

Let's begin by viewing your narrative from three different perspectives, using the powerful tool introduced earlier called *dimostrazione*, the technique that Leonardo da Vinci used while creating masterpieces. The three perspectives are:

▸ An *intellectual* perspective—the Big Idea

▸ An *emotional* perspective—the Story

▸ A *personal* perspective—the Grail

THE BIG IDEA—AN INTELLECTUAL PERSPECTIVE

So what's the Big Idea? The Bates Communications definition of the Big Idea is a single, simple concept so powerful that people will be inspired to remember it and act on it. Think of an elephant on a skateboard: It's big, and it has lots of momentum! You can imagine the Big Idea picking up steam as it moves through your organization.

FIGURE 9.2 | THE BIG IDEA

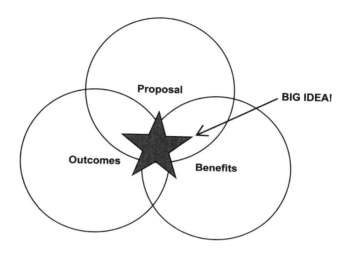

The Big Idea is driven by unique insights and can be found where a proposed solution intersects with its outcomes and benefits (see Figure 9.2). Big Ideas typically focus on making the business more competitive and delivering more value to customers as well as increasing productivity, profitability, and shareholder value.

This is your opportunity to capture what's at the core of your company's truths as expressed by you. Your Big Idea is a laser pointer focusing everyone on what is important. Your words, your business strategy, and your vision for your team, your department, your organization, and your company will all tie back to this simple, powerful message. People will hear *you* as they listen to your passionate, authentic words in your message. The atmosphere of your company will give your Big Idea momentum because your message resonates with what constitutes the atmosphere. When Neil Goldberg uttered the words "Enhance the customer's shopping experience," we knew it was the single most important idea that would make us successful, a vow to carry us through good times and bad. We felt committed to taking action to make it happen. It was a simple message that summed up everything we were about as a company and everything he believed as the leader of our company.

So how do you come up with your single, powerful Big Idea? You probably already have several brewing. Begin by thinking about what your company does that the world wants and needs. Is it a product you produce or a service you provide?

Here are some more useful tips to get started:

1. *It may be helpful to think of the Big Idea as a "future state."* If you are struggling to come up with the essence of what your company does that the world wants and needs, think of the ideal future state for the organization. Do some "what-if" thinking. What if you were completely successful doing what you do 100 percent of the time; how will the world have changed?

2. *In other words, the Big Idea should be a game-changing concept.* It should represent not just a better way to handle a one-off situation but rather something that would change your whole mindset or processes or goals as an organization. It gives your organization a way to overcome issues that have stumped it to date.

3. *The Big Idea should entice your audience into an inquisitive state.* Your audience will want to know more about it; it should provoke intellectual curiosity.

4. *Once you have identified a Big Idea, one important litmus test is the value test.* Is the *value* of the idea clear and undeniable? There should be an emotional component that will excite people. Shortly, we will build on that with a proven tool for giving your Big Idea emotion: *storytelling.*

5. *Finally, in general terms, it should be easy to understand what the results or outcome of the Big Idea would be.* The results should be embedded in the Big Idea "in general terms" because the Big Idea should be condensed to 25 words or less. Remember, the Big Idea isn't powerful unless it's succinct.

Coming up with the Big Idea can be difficult, but keep at it. The key is to keep drilling into the question of "So what?" Explore different possible directions that the receiver could go with the Big Idea, such as various possible benefits relating to profitability, productivity, cost savings, growth, and so on.

Get clear on your Big Idea by writing it down and taking it for a road test with a trusted partner before you go to the larger audience. Someone else's perspective can really help you develop clarity about your Big Idea. The exercises at the end of this chapter will help.

TELL US A STORY, PLEASE!

Now that you have begun to identify your Big Idea, you need a story that brings your idea to life. As our CEO Suzanne Bates has said, "Storytelling is as old as time and as new as the coolest app on your iPhone." At Bates Communications, storytelling is a cornerstone to how we teach people about powerful leadership communication, and nothing is more cutting edge. Stories are the *signal* amid the noise of the digital age! They are the *lighthouse* to the leader looking to help her team navigate the stormy seas of a troubled economy!

Stories speak to people's emotions and can rally excitement. Storytelling also can help you convey your Big Idea in a more comfortable and genuine style of communication.

What happens to people when they tell stories?

▸ They become animated; their eyes light up.

▸ They get excited.

▸ They inject *themselves* into the scene.

▸ They capitalize on the audience interest that they generate by engaging people emotionally.

As a leader, you may sometimes forget that other people would really like to get to know you. They want to know what you stand for and what you're all about. Getting animated and talking about your experiences is important because they want to connect with you as a person.

In large companies, it is impossible to really know everybody as you move into senior leadership, but the people in the organization need to know *you*. Thus, we use storytelling to give your employees, customers, shareholders, and vendors a chance to get to know you and connect with you as their leader. Audiences are *longing* to know you as a person. That's what makes stories such a compelling, rich source of learning. Your own stories are the best stories because they humanize you. You just have to know how to develop them. When Suzanne Bates makes presentations related to her newest book *Discover Your CEO Brand* (McGraw-Hill, 2011), she talks about how we all possess a locked treasure chest of experiences. With the right combination of effort and support, you can learn to unlock that treasure chest and discover your personal brand. You won't believe how much gold has been right under your nose!

Why tell a story?

▶ It's a great way to connect logically and emotionally!

▶ We can speak more conversationally.

▶ We create a reason to keep our audience listening: In this age of BlackBerrys and iPads, it's hard to keep people's attention for more than 5 or 10 minutes.

▶ When the people in our audience hear a story, their brains start saying, "I think I know where this is going . . . ," and they try to fill in the blanks while coming along for the ride. It engages them by pulling them in.

▶ People remember stories more than they remember abstract points in isolation.

Properly structured stories are powerful business communication tools because they put your audience on the edge of their seats and engage their intellectual curiosity (see Figure 9.3).

Storytelling is not entertaining window dressing; it's a high-level leadership communication skill.

FIGURE 9.3 | HOW PEOPLE REMEMBER

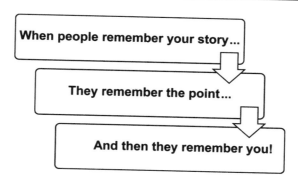

On a personal level, developing stories helps you:

▶ Get in touch with the experiences and lessons that made you who you are

▶ Communicate the behaviors and values you want to drive into the organization

▶ Express values and philosophies important to you that can make your team successful

On an organizational level, developing stories helps leaders:

▶ Drive behaviors down into the organization

▶ Reinforce individual and team behaviors

▶ Motivate and inspire others

▶ Demonstrate connection and awareness

THE BATES STORY STRUCTURE

Back in Exercise 7.1, we introduced you to the Bates Story Structure (see Figure 9.4) as you began to crack the code of your secret sauce. But just as this tool can be very helpful for powerful internal insight, it can be equally powerful as you focus externally on how to move the hearts of your audience. So let's revisit the concept here and go into greater depth.

FIGURE 9.4 | THE BATES STORY STRUCTURE

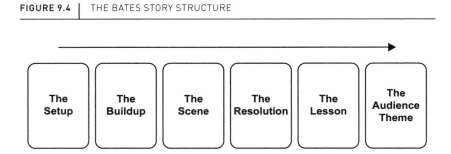

If you follow this formula, ruthlessly eliminate elements of the story that are nice but don't contribute value to its intended purpose, and remain true to each of the six parts, you'll have the key to unlocking that treasure chest. Be sure that your story has a setup, buildup, and conflict that will be resolved during the course of your brief narrative. Don't forget to share the lesson that you learned through resolving the conflict.

Let's consider each step in detail.

The Setup

This is like journalism: We need to establish who, what, when, where, and how very efficiently. If the story is only three minutes or so, this setup piece might literally be roughly three sentences. When should the camera start rolling? Fiction writers use the Latin term *in medias res*, or "in the middle of things," to indicate that almost all present-day stories don't start with the birth of a character; they start at a specific point in the character's life. Think about when the events leading up to your scene *really* began; a story spanning several weeks and months is not very workable in a short speech.

The Buildup

While we build up interest in the story by describing obstacles, difficult odds, or other forms of adversity, we also want to make sure that we're only including elements that will serve a point. Be selective: Think about "nice to know" versus "need to know."

Anton Chekhov, the famous playwright, once said, "If in the first act you have hung a pistol on the wall, then in the following act it must be fired. Otherwise, don't put it there." Every detail of your story needs to pay off. Give your listeners just enough background so they will know what's at stake when we reach the scene.

THE SCENE

In a movie, this might be where the director zooms in for the extreme close-up. It might be Darth Vader in *Star Wars* saying, "Luke, I am your father." It might be Voldemort coming face-to-face in a graveyard with Harry Potter. For your story, you may want to zoom in to catch the details of a key conversation, a sequence of events, or some other critical moment. There may be some tough choices here, so you might have to explore what would be the *best* scene. There often are several possibilities.

THE RESOLUTION

Did you ever go to a movie and find yourself surprised when the ending credits came up? "That's it?" you might hear the audience say quizzically. A story that is really good right up to the end can still disappoint us if we don't have a sense of what the outcome or result was. Don't skim over that! Conflict pulls us in, so we need to know *what happened*, for better or worse. We have to remind some of our coaching clients about that.

THE LESSON

The lesson usually begins with one of the following statements: "What I saw . . . ," "What I learned . . . ," "What became clear to me . . ." There is an "I/me/my" piece to the lesson. This is your personal reflection on what happened in the story. Here you want to avoid simple platitudes along the lines of "Life is hard" or "Take a chance." Go for something a little more specific, nuanced, complex, or multidimensional.

For stories to be successful, you need to position yourself as a *learner* in the story . . . not as the *hero* of the story. Your story certainly can *have* a hero—maybe it's one of your employees or someone else you admire. But your audience will empathize with you far more if you cast yourself as the humble apprentice of life rather than as the conquering champion.

THE AUDIENCE THEME

When we refer to the audience theme, we're talking about a theme that will be interesting and pertinent to your particular audience. The same story could have different themes depending on the audience. The same story might be spun quite differently for vendors than it would be for your employees, for example. However, you should never, ever slant the truth or make something up for effect. If you do, your audience will know or become suspicious and the whole value of storytelling will be lost or discounted. Even worse, your credibility may be in question. All we are suggesting here is that you want to build a relevant bridge from *your* experience and personal learning to the *audience's* interests, needs, hopes, and concerns.

THE GRAIL: YOUR VISION FROM YOUR PERSPECTIVE

Perhaps nothing is more important to your followers than to clearly understand your vision as told from your personal perspective. What matters most—to you? This is what I call the Grail, because you always should be searching for it, clarifying it, and refining it. The Grail is the convergence of your personal truths, your organization's truths, and your Big Idea.

Let me relate a story that will help you as you search for your Grail. It's a story about Jack Dorsey, one of the cofounders of Twitter, a company that has emerged as a social media giant over the last five years. The first tweet was sent in March 2006. Can you guess how many tweets were sent on just one day, five years later? The answer is the whopping total of 171 million tweets! All sent on March 11, 2011, and, as you read this, that amazing number could have very well been doubled or tripled on a recent day! Twitter started off as a head-scratching fad that was mostly popular with teens and early adopters of technology. Now a growing number of organizations and individuals view it as a great way to deliver succinct informative messages to targeted audiences and to create a dialogue with those audiences.

Jack Dorsey is no longer with the company that he cofounded, but his personal story remains an important part of the legends and folklore that define Twitter. Using facts from a *Vanity Fair* interview as well as a story from MediaShift, I'll share the story of Twitter's cofounder. The intention here is for you to see a model of our six-part story structure and imagine how powerful it might be for Twitter's current CEO Dick Costolo to share this story with employees, customers, vendors, or investors. We'll take a look at how Twitter grew from the cofounder's personal story and how Costolo could use the founder's story to help capture the organization's core truths, connect it to his own truths, and energize everyone with his powerful message. Then, we'll make this message even more powerful by condensing it—first into a succinct Big Idea and then into a powerful two-word tagline.

So let's begin with the cofounder's story. This story melds together the aforementioned articles on Dorsey along with some quotes that Shea Bennett of AllTwitter pulled together after listening to Costolo at the Web 2.0 Summit in San Francisco in October 2010.

THE SETUP

Even as a boy, Jack Dorsey was fascinated by shorthand communication across time and space. He was obsessed with taxis and emergency vehicles, especially with how they regularly provided updates to each other and to their central dispatchers about their locations and activities.

Dorsey also loved computer programming. By the age of 15, he was writing code for dispatch routing software—and some of it is still used by taxi companies today!

THE BUILDUP

By early 2006, Dorsey dropped out of New York University and ended up working for a San Francisco start-up called Odeo. At the time, the company was likely going nowhere, but while working on his programming projects and bouncing around between jobs, Dorsey had become intrigued with a Big Idea: What if, by using technology, a person could have the ability to share his or her status and location with others the same way ambulances and taxis do? Imagine being able to easily share a short update with your friends and family.

THE SCENE

So one day Dorsey went to his boss at Odeo to share his big idea. He talked about how taxi communications were like haikus—those short but evocative Japanese poems written in 17 syllables—that are a simple but interesting way to communicate. Dorsey suggested that his company create a service that would allow anyone to write a line or two about him, using a cell phone's keypad, and then transmit that message to anyone who wanted to receive it. Just as he had loved thinking about ambulances and taxis providing constant updates from around a city, this provided a way to fit people in everyday life into that vision.

THE RESOLUTION

Odeo's cofounder, Evan Williams, approved the plan, and Twitter was born. Now six years old, Twitter is one of the three most popular social media platforms at the time of this writing, along with Facebook and LinkedIn. It has over 200 million users, and Google, Facebook, and Microsoft reportedly have been trying to buy the company for more than $8 billion.

THE LESSON

So, to an audience of talented new hires eager to help make Twitter the best and most popular social media platform in a highly competitive field, Costolo might say something like this, "Twitter came to be because of our founder's fascination with real-time, mobile communication. But what really strikes me about his story is that he realized that there is power in simplicity. Just as with a haiku, there is beauty, elegance, boldness, and value in a simply expressed thought that anyone can grasp immediately. Information is power, but information simply communicated is absolutely powerful." Costolo could effectively use the lesson from this story to engage the hearts and minds of an audience of eager new employees.

THE AUDIENCE THEME

Then, to ignite the energy within these talented new employees, he might say, "As of October 2011, we've reached a total of over a quarter of billion tweets per day! We have 50 million daily active users. Our integration with Apple's iPhone has tripled our number of signups, and experts have confirmed our value to be $8 billion.

So what's next for us as a company? We will leverage the power of our secret sauce and outlast Facebook and Google+ because our secret is in our simplicity. Simple is powerful, but it is also hard to perfect. Yet we will pursue perfect simplicity because we have all the potential in the world to connect with every person on the planet . . . and we know the way to do it: simplify."

Do you feel the power of this statement?

THE BIG IDEA

That's an example of how we might construct a Twitter story that CEO Costolo could use to ignite all of his important audiences. What would be the Big Idea that we could derive from it? Well, as it turns out, Twitter revealed a new mission statement in January 2011. Here it is:

To instantly connect people everywhere to what's most important to them.

That's just 11 words . . . or, to put that in Twitter terms, it's 72 characters—significantly shorter than the 140-character maximum for a tweet! Yet there's no question that it is a powerful and ambitious statement—one that likely took hours and hours to craft.

Let's reverse engineer the Big Idea here and take a close look at the key words. This will model the thought process:

▶ *Instantly* captures the real-time immediacy of a Twitter message—one of the primary reasons why this medium has become so interesting to people and organizations looking to track the elusive buzz that ebbs and flows around people and products. It's a brilliant tool to "listen" as you "tell" others your position.

▶ *Connect people* brings us right back to the founder's initial mission—helping people connect in a very simple and easily accessible way. Twitter is looking to remind people that this is still an intimate form of communication, albeit an electronic one. This is a differentiating and inspiring part of the Big Idea.

▶ *Everywhere* is a very significant word. This new mission statement "hints at the growing speculation that Twitter will be embracing location and locale as a new means to drive engagement and even revenue," according to www.twitterati.com. If so, then *everywhere* is *bold foreshadowing of a future state* for Twitter—an important element of any Big Idea. But the word *everywhere* also encompasses the idea of an increased international presence as well as, say, showcasing the fact that you could easily be tweeting from Hawaii or the local zoo. Twitter will be everywhere.

▶ *To what's most important to them* is a compelling phrase that combines several elements of a Big Idea. The phrase implies personal freedom and choice, and total control over both. Freedom and choice are two of the most revered human conditions. Who wouldn't be moved by this thought? And if it's "important to them," it's something people will not only want to have, it is something they will need.

Taken as a whole, this Big Idea seems to capture the essence, the "secret sauce," of a company that is growing exponentially and of an organization that is ambitiously and strategically moving beyond personal chat into the grand realm of information and commerce. The Rally Cry "to instantly connect people everywhere to what's most important to them" delivered powerfully by the CEO as part of a well-planned communication strategy could energize everyone in and around Twitter and marshal their collective actions to give the company an enormous competitive advantage. But why stop here . . .

WHAT'S HAPPENING?

Twitter also held true to its belief in simplicity when the company recently revised its tagline to—"What's happening?" The old tagline was "What are you doing?" That was sensible enough when the microblogging company's primary focus was on personal status updates, but cofounder Biz Stone told the AFP News Agency in November 2009 that times had changed. "People, organizations, *and* businesses quickly began leveraging the open nature of the network to share anything they wanted, completely ignoring the original question, seemingly on a quest to both ask and answer a different, and more immediate question." That question? *What's happening?*

"What's happening" is a terrific Rally Cry for Twitter. Just two words—and a mere 17 characters—"What's happening?" is the question that now appears above the status update box when you log in at Twitter. Simple but also very powerful because it has a double or even triple meaning. Take out that question mark, and you can use it to describe Twitter's mission. They're all about the immediacy of what's happening *right now* . . . and Twitter itself is a very happening trend. And, it's *beautifully* simple, just like those emergency vehicle communications that inspired cofounder Jack Dorsey in his boyhood days.

So "What's happening?" could be considered the Grail. Despite its brevity, it does pay homage to Dorsey's vision of simplicity and connection . . . but it also captures the personal perspective of Costolo, whose mission is to move the company into the larger and more lucrative marketplace of information and commerce.

That's some pretty good heavy lifting for just 17 characters!

IMPORTANT VENUES FOR YOUR POWERFUL MESSAGE

Once you've crafted your Big Idea, Rally Cry, or tagline, you have to make sure that it's heard. To say something that excites people, spread your message and tell your compelling story to as many audiences and in as many venues as possible. Remember, just when you are getting sick of hearing yourself say it, the people who hear it are *just starting to believe it.*

Here are some tips we have found most effective in spreading your energized message:

▶ *Talk about what it will mean to become one of the most admired companies* in the industry, and for that matter, in the Fortune 100.

▶ *Create "imagine that . . ." or "what if . . ."* scenarios with examples and talking points that resonate powerfully with every employee inside your company and the most important stakeholders outside your company.

▶ *Roll out these messages strategically*—meaning roll out the right messages at the right time, in the right forum, and by the right person.

▶ *Prepare interesting, employee-friendly materials* (e.g., key messages, fact sheets, Q&A) for your leaders and managers to use when communicating with their individual teams.

▶ *Collect, write, and develop material for live, written, broadcast, and online media* based on success stories, including employees sharing their "point of view" through the channels you have set up.

▶ *Communicate through influencers.* Get conversations going among those who are powerful shapers of the shared viewpoint. We'll explore this concept more thoroughly in Chapter 10.

▶ *Coach the key leaders on the teams* (e.g., executives, project managers, and, most important, the Alpha Dogs) to deliver the message, invite feedback, and be utterly comfortable, confident, and authentic, winning trust and engagement in all their interactions. We will get further into this in Chapter 11.

IGNITE YOUR CULTURE'S ENERGY

CEOs like Dick Costolo value speed. In many cases they can be like cheetahs, focusing their attention on the weakest gazelle in the pack. Think Jack Welch and his differentiation practice, aka *20-70-10*. That works well for a cheetah looking for its next meal, but as a strategy to ignite the energy in your culture, it could be a big mistake.

Ironically, most leaders miss this next step. So in the next chapter we will concentrate on how you broadcast your Rally Cry—efficiently and effectively. There is a very important group of people who are just waiting to charge out of the gate armed with your message. This is where you should focus your gaze—first!

WRITE A PERSONAL STORY

[For all of the exercises that follow, you will want to use a separate note-book or scratch pad. The work you will do in these three exercises will require multiple edits, and it is useful to reflect on the iterations of ideas that occur over time.]

In this chapter, you read a story about Jack Dorsey and Twitter. That story revolved around a few turning points—getting immersed in the real-time communication of ambulances and taxis, then making a cognitive leap to applying the same concepts toward connecting people with technology, and finally finding someone to fund the venture. What a turn of events! Jack Dorsey had been a college dropout bouncing from job to job, and suddenly he became the pioneer behind a company that has transformed social media.

What was a turning point in your life journey? Or maybe it was an instructive failure or some sort of startling discovery. Regardless, the goal is to begin to unlock your treasure chest of experiences. So now we're going to focus on how you can use stories to make your message come alive! Developing a personal story will also help you with creating a Big Idea and a Rally Cry.

We're going to focus first on helping you find the powerful *point* in your story and putting some structure and discipline around the story to make it economical and efficient in its telling. Here's how it works:

▶ Read the categories below. These are categories of stories that our experience has found to be particularly rich areas to explore. They can relate to your life *or* career. Reflect on each category before moving on to the next. Go inside yourself, go inside your memory bank, and allow whatever wants to come to the surface to bubble up. Don't edit it—just let it rise.

▶ Personal challenges, difficult decisions, choices, hurdles, obstacles that you've faced in your life or career.

▶ Startling events, major changes, turning points.

▶ Embarrassments, awkward situations, dumb ideas, failures.

▶ Inspiring people, remarkable achievements, memorable events that you've witnessed.

▶ Discoveries, travel stories, interesting people you've met, places you've been.

Now revisit the categories above. As you reflect, jot down a handful of words that describe what bubbled up for each category. Choose one of those ideas to work on and develop as your story. What have you thought of that you haven't thought about for years? Some of your story ideas might not be appropriate for business, but don't worry about that right now. You won't have to have an idea for every category, but try to zero in on an idea that you'd like to explore.

Here are some tips how:

▶ Don't feel that you have to understand what the point of the story is just yet.

▶ Look at the story idea that most interests you—the one that you really want to explore to see if it really *is* a story.

▶ Consider using the story that seems the most interesting or painful or poignant or fun.

Use the six-part story structure as described in this chapter to give your story structure and to align it with an audience that you have in mind. In summary, here is that structure again:

▶ *The setup.* The who, what, when, and where of the story, told succinctly.

▶ *The buildup.* The conflict, problem, or challenge that must be faced.

- *The scene.* The "snapshot in time" where we drill into a specific turn of events, such as a critical conversation or sequence of events.

- *The resolution.* The outcome of the story: How was the problem or challenge resolved?

- *The lesson.* What did you learn from this experience? How did it change you?

- *The audience theme.* How does what you learned relate to what you want the listener of the story to take away from it?

Exercise 9.2

CRAFT YOUR BIG IDEA

Now, just as Twitter did when crafting their mission statement, take a stab at capturing your Big Idea. The goal is to boil down the current description of your high-energy organization into a Big Idea of 25 words or less. Here are some helpful reminders:

1. It may be helpful to think of the Big Idea as a *future state*. If you were completely successful doing what you do 100 percent of the time, how will the world have changed?

2. The Big Idea should be a *game-changing concept*. It would change your whole mindset or processes or goals as an organization.

3. The Big Idea should entice your audience into an *inquisitive state*. It should provoke intellectual curiosity.

4. Is the *value* of the idea *clear and undeniable?* There should be an emotional component that will excite people.

5. We should understand in general terms *what the results or outcome of the Big Idea would be*.

To develop an initial Big Idea, try the following:

▸ *Brainstorm.* Write down the key words and phrases that come to mind, especially those that have materialized through exploration of your personal truths as well as the other truths that have emerged from key stakeholders.

▸ *Prioritize.* Look critically at your list of words and phrases; then stack-rank them according to which are most important.

▶ *Construct.* Try to build a 25-word or less Big Idea, being sure to tie together your top words or phrases.

▶ *Digest.* Let your draft sit over a few nights, allowing your subconscious an opportunity to work on the Big Idea.

▶ *Revisit.* Look anew at the Big Idea. Does it really capture what your organization is all about? Are you excited by it? Have you left anything out? Could anything else be taken out to make it more simple and powerful?

▶ *Test.* Once you are comfortable with it, try your Big Idea out on others.

One last note: As we said earlier, simple is hard! Crafting a Big Idea—or boiling a complex story down into a succinct six-step, three-minute story—is no easy feat. Give it a try, but I would encourage you to enlist expert assistance. An executive coach or strategic communications consultant can make a world of difference when you're striving to develop the most powerful, resonating messages for your important audiences.

CREATE YOUR RALLY CRY

As I said throughout this chapter, simple is hard. In Exercise 9.1, you've written a story that you should be able to tell in about three minutes. In Exercise 9.2, you crafted a Big Idea that is 25 words or less. Now I'm asking you to do the heaviest lifting of all: Create a Rally Cry that captures who you are—your special sauce—in as few words as possible. It should be an extremely succinct phrase, such as "Think Different" or "Just Do It." As another example, remember that Twitter came up with "What's Happening?"

This is a big challenge, but imagine how powerful it would be to nail this one.

Here are some tips:

- ▶ *Reflect on your personal stories.* The most powerful ones may have a theme or lesson that will inspire your Rally Cry.

- ▶ *Consider your Big Idea.* Is there a phrase that takes the Big Idea and boils it down to its very simple essence?

- ▶ *Create first; judge later.* Turn off your internal editor and just run wild with whatever comes to mind. Sometimes a crazy idea or a joke precedes the development of the Rally Cry.

- ▶ *Get expert assistance if you need it.* If you get stuck, turn to a communications expert for help. Sometimes getting an outside perspective is helpful, especially from those who work on these issues all the time.

CHAPTER **10**

Save the "Saved"

One-fifth of the people are against everything all the time.
—ROBERT F. KENNEDY, FORMER U.S.
SENATOR AND ATTORNEY GENERAL

Inspired by his father's exemplary career, Paul Muench opted to become a schoolteacher. Proving that the apple doesn't fall all that far from the tree, Paul, too, is a revered and beloved teacher. He is a peer leader among the faculty in one of the top school systems in the state of New York. Recently Paul told me a story. When he started teaching high school social studies, he became discouraged. In his class of 25 students, the problem was that he was unable to get 4 of those kids charged up about learning despite his best efforts.

Naturally, he turned to his dad for advice. His father sagely nodded as Paul vented about that quartet of apathetic teens. Then he asked Paul an interesting question. "How much time are you spending on these four kids in relation to the top four in your class?"

Paul thought for a moment. Then he said, "At least three times as much time."

Paul's dad smiled and looked down. Then he looked directly into Paul's eyes. "That's the problem, Paul. *Save the saved* first. Then you will have peer disciples who will help you save the rest."

Paul's dad had learned this lesson from his own experience. To energize his classroom, he had to energize the top kids in his class first, and then they would help energize the rest. Starting with the least engaged kids was a waste of time. They would be the most difficult to change—

maybe impossible. In the meantime, your top kids end up becoming disillusioned: They had come to class ready to learn, and what had they received in return? Little to no attention.

The significance for business leaders is profound. Your disciples are the top 5 to 20 percent of your people who are yearning to understand your vision. They long to take your compelling future state of the current organization and make it reality. They are the self-motivated stars on the edge of their seats, just waiting to be charged up by your clear, simple, and powerful message. They are eager to charge forward armed with your vision and their peer-leading capabilities.

Most important, they are often uniquely able to broadcast your message in a powerful way because they are the high achievers. Others in your organization respect them. They are the ones who always excel and always challenge themselves to be the best. When you focus your time and attention on them, you are investing in your *own* success. When peak performers believe in you, they will walk through fire to live up to or exceed your expectations. They are the winners on your team. If yours is a high-performance culture, then these are the people who will not tolerate team members who lack commitment. They will act to get them on board and push them forward. Soon, those who remain disengaged and who lag behind become outliers. They either quit or become so countercultural that you can pick them out and remove them yourself.

The fact that most leaders overlook the enormous extra value they have in these gem assets is the most puzzling paradox in leadership today. These are the "vital few" that leaders must focus on first if they are to quickly move the needle in the direction of their goals.

THE PARETO PRINCIPLE

In 1906, Vilfredo Pareto discovered that 80 percent of the peas in his garden came from 20 percent of the peapods. As an economist and engineer in Italy, he was curious to learn why. As he pursued his curiosity, he began to uncover other incidences where the ratio seemed to apply. For instance, he learned that 80 percent of the land in Italy at the time was owned by 20 percent of the population. Recognizing the general significance of this phenomenon, business management consultant Joseph Juran further developed the principle and applied it to business, concluding that 80 percent of the *effects* come from 20 percent of the *causes*. He named the principle after Pareto, and it is now commonly known as the Pareto principle, or the 80-20 rule.

There are many fascinating examples of this rule:

▶ Just 20 percent of the world's population controls roughly 82 percent of world income.

▶ Microsoft discovered that fixing the top 20 percent of reported bugs stopped 80 percent of the errors and crashes that occurred.

▶ One-fifth of the U.S. population uses four-fifths of the health-care resources.

In management, the Pareto principle is often taken to imply that since 20 percent of your people produce 80 percent of the results, for instance in sales, you should focus the majority of your time on the top 20 percent. While this is debatable, the Pareto principle is definitely an important concept in leadership communications. As a leader who is committed to spreading your powerful message, you should focus first on the 20 percent of your leadership team who will leverage your message to maximum effect, spreading it quickly and effectively.

Have you heard the cliché "Don't preach to the converted"? That does *not* apply when you set out to spread your powerful message like wildfire through your organization. Preach your powerful message to the ones who are already true believers. They will then preach in kind! The cascading effect will pick up speed as it travels through your atmosphere, like the elephant on a skateboard that we talked about in the previous chapter. Speed is a crucial advantage in business. It's also a primary performance measure for CEOs. How fast did he turn the company around? How quickly did he create a rise in the stock value? How quickly did he get the new innovative product to market? How fast did he get the marketing strategy implemented? The best are the fastest. And the best know how to leverage the talent that resides within their ranks to increase velocity through powerful communication.

START WITH FACE-TO-FACE
COMMUNICATION . . . THEN WORK BACKWARD

We are living in an age of exponential change. The rate of change is increasing faster and faster. This adds a dimension of complexity to leading change that is not solved simply, and certainly not by electronic communication alone. In fact, ironically, in business today, more than in the past, effective in-person communication is more of a competitive advantage because so many leaders today rely on other more efficient, less effective forms of communication. Yes, e-mail is a great tool to quickly share information—and it does have the advantage of speed—but it is a poor tool for translating emotion. Purpose and passion are very difficult to transfer via e-mail.

When we teach communication at Bates Communications, we use the following simple sentence to teach the importance of emphasis and inflection to ensure that your audience understands your point:

I did not say you were going to get a raise this year.

Take a moment and say the sentence out loud, stressing the italicized word in the sentence each time:

I did not say you were going to get a raise this year.

I did *not* say you were going to get a raise this year.

I did not *say* you were going to get a raise this year.

I did not say *you* were going to get a raise this year.

I did not say you were going to get a *raise* this year.

I did not say you were going to get a raise *this* year.

See how the meaning changes? The written form of this sentence can be interpreted at least six different ways depending on the person reading it and his perception. It is the person writing it—and who is trying to communicate something important—whose intent matters.

We tell our leaders to start with face-to-face communication and work backward. Your most important messages *must* be communicated in person, in one-on-one conversations *first!* This is the *gold standard* because in-person, one-to-one conversations allow for focus, nuance, and impact of both verbal *and* nonverbal cues.

LEADERSHIP COMMUNICATION RULE #1. *THE MORE CRITICAL THE MESSAGE, THE CLOSER YOU MUST BE TO YOUR AUDIENCE*

As a leader, it's important to start with one-to-one, face-to-face communication with your key disciples. Make sure they get the message. Then take one step backward for the critical next step: one-to-*group* communication. One-to-group communication could be in the form of a "road show" or a "town meeting" where you have employees in a room live and where they have the opportunity to interact with you in person. When you have hit all possible important groups live and in person with your message, then you can take one step further back. As you'll see later in this chapter with a compelling example about FedEx, communicating one-to-group via broadcast media is a very useful tool when your leaders and key players are geographically spread across the country or the world. One-to-group can be in the form of a live video feed or an interactive webcast. Again, however, frequent, deliberate, and in-person interaction with your key disciples is imperative. One step further back is the conference call. And furthest back from the gold standard is the broadcast e-mail.

Interestingly, most leaders start—and end—with these last two methods to channel their important messages. These two methods alone *do not* effectively cascade your message. Your message gets minimized to words only, while your audience stays focused only briefly. The message gets lost and is more likely to be misinterpreted. Over a remarkably short period of time, it gets forgotten. Only if all the other steps are completed effectively will the broadcast e-mail become a useful means of *reinforcing* the message, because the recipients have *already heard the message from you, in person, as the leader. And your message was understood because the audience heard and felt your passion.* Your in-person delivery of the message charged up the people in your audience. They got the picture. As one executive leader we've worked with put it, "Calls and videoconferences are okay for sound bites, but they don't let you delve into an issue or build the personal relationships that really help get things done."

The essential point is to establish a consistent, personalized communication plan, message, and style. Once you have focused on the gold standard and energized your disciples, make sure you have a regular schedule for group communication so that you are reinforcing the messages that are cascading throughout your organization. This schedule should be a means for ensuring that you are heard directly, and it should allow for dialogue and information sharing. Consistency builds trust and clarity. Be disciplined. Don't reschedule one-to-group meetings unless absolutely necessary.

LEADERSHIP COMMUNICATION RULE #2.
REINFORCE YOUR GROUP COMMUNICATION WITH CONSTANT INDIVIDUAL COMMUNICATION

Whenever the opportunity presents itself to reiterate the message—whether in a one-on-one meeting, a group meeting, or another setting—seize the opportunity. Any form of personalized touch amplifies and solidifies your message as well as your passion behind it.

A simple, powerful tool that Neil Goldberg uses frequently is the personal handwritten note. In this age of electronic communication, a simple handwritten note conveys a message more powerfully than ever. First, the recipient of Neil's note intuits that both he and the message must be important if Neil handwrote it. "*I* must be important if he took the time to write to me," he thinks when receiving the note, imagining how busy a CEO must be. The thought process continues: "I must do *something* in return. I know! I'll be sure to endorse Neil and his message whenever I have the opportunity!" Truly effective. And a brilliant use of an age-old powerful communication tool—the simple handwritten note.

Max Dupree, author of the seminal book on leadership *Leadership Is an Art*, emphasizes the importance of saying your message over and over and over until it is *right! right! right!* The more you *say* your powerful message as a leader, the more you personally *understand* your message, the more powerful your communication becomes over time. As you repeat your message in front of person after person and group after group, the essence of your message will remain, but your style, your delivery, and the words will change. They will change to make your message authentic and very powerful, because you will have finally internalized the message so deeply that it becomes an extension of your personal truths.

COMMUNICATE WITH PONZI POWER

Ponzi schemes are illegal and have no legitimate place in business. They are tantalizing to early investors, however, because of the power of exponential growth. Comparably, if we replace dollar investment with communication investment, this scheme becomes enormously valuable in business. As a leader, when you convey your message to five people, who are then marshaled into action and they convey it to five people each, who are then marshaled into action . . . it is not very long before your message has powerfully impacted your whole organization *and* the value of repetition is realized most by the early conveyors. And who are these early conveyors? They're your top 5 to 20 percent performers. Enormous power!

I learned this firsthand with our Leadership Development Institute, where we quantified our disciples were the top 18 percent of the leaders from our programs. Armed with new knowledge on how to become the best leaders they could be, they committed to doing so by acting on their newly declared truths. They were the courageous minority, and their power drove our business. When it came to our company initiative to penetrate metropolitan New York, we placed the primary burden on their shoulders. About half of them were capable of communicating powerfully. These were the elite. Like the military, they were our special forces. We concluded that if we were to succeed, we would have to focus on these key disciples to spread the message and marshal action exponentially. When these few understood the direction, bought into the strategic plan, and acted to carry it out, our Big Idea picked up momentum in a hurry.

CHANGE LEADERSHIP AT FEDEX

Change is constant in business today. Like the best ice hockey players, leaders must "skate ahead of the puck" by envisioning opportunity and guiding their organizations through significant change to seize the opportunity before anyone else. Change management is difficult. There is little margin for error given the enormous capital costs involved and the scarce resources available. Leaders must have extraordinary skill when it comes to bringing people together around a common purpose, marshaling their collective actions to drive the change successfully to completion.

FedEx CEO Fred Smith is a great example of a leader who manages change effectively . . . who seemingly thrives on it, in fact. Consider all the innovations that FedEx has rolled out over the last three decades:

- ▶ It was the first to use bar-code labeling in ground transportation in 1981.

- ▶ It began a PC-based automated shipping system in 1984.

- ▶ It was the first to let customers track shipments online in 1994.

- ▶ Then it made it possible for customers to create their own shipping labels in 1996.

- ▶ Its emphasis on IT innovation is so profound that CIO Rob Carter was named one of the "100 most creative people in business" by *Fast Company* magazine in 2010.

As CIO.com reported, FedEx underwent a massive reorganization in January 2000. The company consolidated four of its five subsidiaries under the name of FedEx while moving IT, sales, and marketing under the banner of FedEx Corporate. As always with the company, the end game of all this upheaval focused on the customer. The goal was to give clients one point of access to sales, customer service, automation systems, and billing.

People *always* resist change. Fred Smith, Rob Carter, and FedEx had the wisdom to realize that communication is the master key to unlocking that resistance. According to the CIO.com article, FedEx implemented the use of "FXTV" to connect company members worldwide with live broadcasts. FedEx piped programming right into employee desktops. "We were informed of what was happening very early on," one employee recalled. "All the steps were laid out clearly through e-mail and FXTV. Even when I wasn't impacted directly, I still knew what was happening throughout the company." While it wasn't plausible for such a large enterprise to meet the Bates gold standard of face-to-face communication with all managers, the broadcasts were the next best thing. "People in my organization think FXTV is the greatest thing in the world because it allows them to get information directly from senior management and that makes a big difference," IT manager Brodie Johnson said.

The CIO.com article didn't mention the Pareto principle by name . . . but it didn't have to. Check out this quote from consultant Susan Annunzio as she reflected on the presence of "change agents" within corporations: "I call it the 20-60-20 rule," she said. "Twenty percent of your people are inner-directed high achievers. At the other end are the 20 percent I call 'the miserable.' Ninety percent of change-management dollars are wasted trying to motivate this group. The key is the 60 percent in the middle. You have to get them to imitate the achievers, to become your allies and agents of change."

Starting from the top down, FedEx focused on keeping people informed and asking for feedback. Ultimately, the company overcame the resistance and continued to wow vendors with extremely responsive problem solving . . . and FedEx hit its goal of implementing this seismic change in just six months!

A NEW CHAPTER IN THE TEACHING OF WRITING

When embarking on a change initiative, leaders often understand that selecting the right people to plan and implement the change is priority one. Yet they often overlook or underrate the importance of the right communication strategy, the right message, and the right leaders out front communicating the message powerfully and effectively. The best plans and implementation strategy are necessary but not sufficient. The secret to making a successful change and driving your business forward is selecting the right leaders to communicate the right message in the right way to the right audiences at the right time.

Here's a case in point. Several years ago, Dr. Phil Martin noticed a nagging issue in his school district in central New York. While students possessed good aptitude and had performed well on state assessments, their writing composition skills lagged behind other language arts skills.

Martin took action. The administrative staff worked in conjunction with one of his premier middle school English teachers to conduct a study, identify a root cause of the discrepancy, and create a plan of action.

Curiously, the study revealed that the lag in writing composition skills of the students was caused in large part by teacher preparation programs at institutions of higher education. For every training course in writing, there were four in reading! In addition, the staff studied the generalists—the elementary school teachers—who had teaching responsibility for the gamut of the curriculum: language arts, math, social studies, and science. Obeying the law of human nature, these elementary school teachers often devoted more instruction time on a daily basis to topics where their comfort level was highest. As a third strike, elementary school instruction across the country has placed emphasis on reading and mathematics. Thus, writing often received short shrift.

Dr. Martin knew that mandates for classroom instructional change are typically insufficient, especially when most of the instruction occurs behind closed doors. It is only when leadership and a cadre of inspired colleagues lead the way that true change in classroom instruction occurs. In recognition of these factors, Dr. Martin looked to one of the district's most talented and influential middle school English teachers to take on the new role of *writing resource teacher*. This individual would have the districtwide responsibility of working with the elementary teaching staff in implementing a richer writing component in its instructional program.

The new writing resource teacher was impassioned by a vision for teaching writing and in turn enlisted the assistance of a Columbia University professor who specialized in the art of teaching writing. Once immersed in the art herself, the writing resource teacher "recruited" 10 of the best, most enthusiastic teachers within the elementary teaching ranks. They were asked not only to participate in the program but also to serve as trainers for the remainder of the teaching staff. In essence, these teachers became disciples of the writing resource teacher. The writing resource teacher and the 10 recruited teachers held training workshops after school hours in addition to morning discussion groups. Moreover, the writing resource teacher *modeled* the art of teaching writing in the classrooms for all elementary teachers. The 10 recruited teachers invited *other* teachers into their classrooms to observe the process in action. These morning discussion groups, after-school training sessions, and classroom demonstrations—along with a formal commitment on the part of the school district at large—helped ease the reluctance of other teachers and gave them encouragement to effectively implement the program within all classrooms.

Without Dr. Martin's decision to begin with the right peer leader, his vision for curriculum reform may have taken years to become a reality, or worse, may have fallen flat on its face. A well-run school system is a function of effective leaders and their savvy use of effective communication. In this case, Dr. Martin was a leader who understood the speed and power of working with the top echelon of teachers as disciples to infuse a new program within the general curriculum. Education reform is perhaps the most critical area where effective leadership is needed in America today, and an area where more effective leadership communication can drive faster results.

TALENT AND A REVAMPING OF EXPECTANCY THEORY

Expectancy theory emphasizes the need for organizations to relate rewards directly to performance and to ensure that the rewards provided are those deserved and wanted by the recipients.

—WIKIPEDIA

In today's postrecession environment, companies are operating with pared-back workforces. Picked to the bone, companies are placing more burden than ever on the best-of-the-best people who remain. A focus on results and earnings in the best cases—or simply survival in other cases—has burned out many leaders who were "A" players but who have been driven to unsustainable levels of output. We see this time and again with the vast majority of our client companies. Some organizations truly fail to save the "saved"—it sometimes seems they hand an anchor to a man trying to stay afloat!

In companies that have misidentified their leadership talent and thus have an inordinate amount of mediocre performers leading that lean workforce, the burden on the elite few is even greater. These leaders are swimming upstream against a rapid and rising current.

At the same time, compensation and rewards have become commoditized when attempting to retain or attract talent. Early into the recession, companies learned that offering competitive salaries, titles, and rewards for results in the form of bonuses and options could help retain and attract the best. Yes, these enticements are important and necessary, but they are no longer sufficient. As a human resources executive with the good fortune of having worked in companies with great people and extraordinary leaders, I can tell you that it is imperative that the components of compensation are aligned with the strategic goals of the organization.

But what if great performance leads to the wrong outcomes? What if disciples don't understand what the desired outcomes really are? What really aligns actions?

Back in the 1960s, Victor Vroom devised expectancy theory. Here is a simplified version of it:

▶ People develop perceptions about whether a given level of *effort* will result in reaching a level of desired *performance*.

▶ People also develop perceptions about whether that level of *performance* will lead to a desired *outcome*.

This all makes sense. If people perceive that their hard work doesn't lead to a desired performance level, they won't want to work as hard. And what if they perform at a high level, only to be "rewarded" with an outcome of more work to do? This can have a definite negative impact on effort and performance.

The problem lies with the traditional notion of expectancy theory (see Figure 10.1). Often the "desired outcome" is defined purely as individual gains in the form of pay increases, promotions, and recognitions. Don't get me wrong. Components of compensation must be aligned with strategic goals. Salaries and other extrinsic benefits must be competitive. However, I can also confidently state that winning the race for talent today all boils down to this: Winners want to be on winning teams. They want to win. Expectancy theory today means winning . . . and sharing the fruits of victory. That is the powerful desired outcome—maybe not for all employees . . . but definitely for those who flourish and drive results at high-energy organizations.

FIGURE 10.1 | EXPECTANCY THEORY

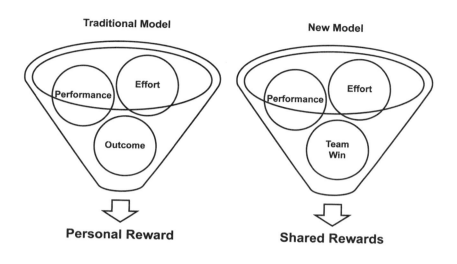

THE THREE COMMON DENOMINATORS OF RECRUITMENT AND RETENTION

In business today, recruiting and retaining the best talent result in an enormous competitive advantage for those who do both well. My experience clearly indicates there are three common denominators to the companies and their cultures that excel at attracting and retaining top leadership talent. These denominators are:

▶ A CEO leader who seeks input from the team and knows how to inspire and motivate through communication

▶ A team of extraordinary executive leaders who share similar values

▶ A high-performance culture that wins

In their book *Hard Facts, Dangerous Half-Truths & Total Nonsense: Profiting from Evidence-Based Management,* Jeffrey Pfeffer and Robert Sutton highlight the vital importance of seeking out disciples deeper in your organization. "We can't find a shred of evidence that it is better to have just a few alpha dogs at the top and to treat everyone else as inferior. Rather, the best performance comes in organizations where as many people as possible are treated as top dogs. If you want people to keep working together and learning together, it is better to grant prestige to many rather than few, and to avoid big gaps between who gets the most and least rewards and kudos." They go on to conclude that "rigorous studies DO imply that great people make great organizations."

In his model of situational leadership, Ken Blanchard categorizes "great people" in organizations as *D-4s,* meaning Development Level 4, aka *self-reliant achievers.* Self-reliant achievers are also sometimes called *peak performers.* They are your potential disciples. For anyone familiar with Blanchard's model, this is the goal in the development cycle. According to the model, there are four basic types of employee:

- ▶ *Enthusiastic beginners,* who are low in competence but high in commitment

- ▶ *Disillusioned learners,* who are still relatively low in competence and also low in commitment

- ▶ *Reluctant contributors,* who are relatively high in competence but low in commitment

- ▶ *Peak performers,* who are high in competence *and* commitment

Continually diagnosing where your people are in the development cycle and flexing your leadership style to meet their specific needs are steps that are paramount to your ability as a leader to develop D-4s, those self-reliant achievers and peak performers. Ironically, though, these folks often remain below the radar precisely because they are so reliable! You can delegate to them and forget about them. These self-sufficient employees allow you to focus your scarce time on other important issues, knowing that the D-4s will take good care of the projects, tasks, and areas of your business for which they are responsible. However, these are the very people who deserve your attention most! They *yearn* to be recognized and challenged further. Seek them out. They are your potential disciples too.

"BALL" OF ENERGY

Charlie Ball was a large, quiet man. When I took over the Corroc Division of Burrows Paper Corporation, I often walked the shop floor, and I always noticed Charlie. He might be helping someone learn a tip or a trick about one of our sophisticated printing presses, or he could be responding to one of the younger members of our team who was shouting out to Charlie for help while setting a knife on a multimillion-dollar Bobst die cutter. Charlie clearly had that referent power and expert power that I discussed in the Alpha Dogs chapter. He was someone whom everyone knew, respected, and cherished for his ability and willingness to help and to teach. He was a magnet for me. Over time, Charlie and I built a strong relationship. He trusted me and I him.

At the time of my arrival, the Corroc Division was bleeding cash. Soon after taking over the division, I learned its ugly little secret: The division was gushing cash at a rate of $300,000 a month—enough to bankrupt the *parent* company within a year without drastic action. It was the worst-case scenario. Every clamshell container for encasing Big Macs that we manufactured for McDonald's *lost* a fraction of a cent. The more we produced, the more we lost! Sales were increasing, and losses were causing a serious cash breach. Never in my career before nor since have I had to deal with the confusing feelings that come with that kind of situation—where increasing sales create increased losses. Talk about great performance failing to lead to a desired outcome! I had to act quickly.

The plan was two pronged. We had to lobby for a price increase with McDonald's and reduce labor costs while *increasing* production and improving quality. The clock was ticking. Besides my leadership team, there were three people whom I knew from my time on the floor that I had to get on board if this plan was to have any chance for success. Obviously, Charlie was one.

When I went onto the floor and pulled Charlie aside, he knew immediately the matter was dire. "Charlie, I need your help. We are on the verge of disaster." *I paused. I distinctly remember the look in Charlie's eyes. He was looking directly into mine, and I knew he could sense my fear and my determination.* "But I think this could also be the beginning of enormous opportunity for all of us if we turn this thing around."

I then went on to explain the situation. Given the quantities that McDonald's was buying, I knew that it did not have immediate options for an alternative supply, even if it wanted one. So I knew with some confidence we would succeed at getting the price increase we desperately needed. I also knew that McDonald's planned to roll out a whole new line of sandwiches—the ultimately ill-fated Arch Deluxe—and had decided to use our clamshells. If we were able to produce these clamshells efficiently and move the cost needle a fraction of a penny in the right direction, a huge loss could turn into a huge profit almost immediately.

Charlie was one of three key people on our team who could help make this happen. After our conversation, he left me impassioned with a spirit that I have seldom witnessed. I'll never forget it. He was a man determined to answer the call, and he began to rally his peer troops immediately after I had the critical call-to-action meeting with everyone. Charlie took my message and helped marshal the actions of everyone to make the needed changes. We won. Over the next 12 months we not only stopped the bleeding, we turned the division cash positive in total for the year. Over the following three years, the Corroc Division was contributing positive cash on a monthly basis at a consistently higher rate until it ultimately became the most profitable division in the company as measured by contribution to corporate. At the end of my fifth year I was named president of the overall corporation, and for that I credit Charlie and the many remarkable employees who worked tirelessly to turn a seemingly dire situation into an enormous win.

The real learning came from what followed. We had done far more than solve a pressing business problem. We found that the entire team became closer. The lesson from this story was that when you rally the key troops and win, the winning becomes a habit. It's addictive!

CONTAGIOUS IS A GOOD WORD

We all share a desire to be inspired. Kiran Bir Sethi founded a groundbreaking school in India called the Riverside School. She gave a riveting talk at a TED conference in India, which I recommend that you check out at www.ted.com. The theme of the school is teaching leadership and "infecting" children with the "I can" bug. Inspired children who learn the concepts take important issues into their own hands, lead other young people, and even educate and incent their parents into action. Yes, the children become self-motivated to lead adults! According to Sethi, there are three steps in each child's journey at Riverside School:

▶ Aware: See the change.

▶ Enable: Be the change.

▶ Empower: Lead the change.

In an incredibly powerful and poignant example, Sethi describes how she taught children in her class the *concepts* relating to child labor, and the concerns surrounding the issue. But this was abstract and inefficient. So she brought them to a factory and had them spend a day rolling incense sticks. They learned firsthand what it was like to work as a child in difficult conditions. They didn't just "know" that child labor was unfair or wrong; they could feel it in their very being! Then they set out to change the world and took steps toward convincing leaders that something had to be done.

In the process, Sethi emphasizes the word *contagious.* "Even in the times of H1N1, I like the word!" she says. "Laughter is contagious. Passion is contagious. Inspiration is contagious."

Using your personal energy and making inspiration contagious while taking your disciples on the same journey—aware, enable, empower— are the goals of your communication with them.

In the words of Kiran Bir Sethi: "Feel—Imagine—Do!"

LEADERSHIP COMMUNICATION RULE #3. *ALWAYS FOCUS ON YOUR AUDIENCE'S AGENDA FIRST, THEN YOUR OWN*

In communicating with your disciples, the most important thing is to focus on *their* agenda first and then your own. This is a fundamental of effective business communication.

Your message should always start with what your audience cares about most. This is why you took the time to query the key players in your organization. If your words don't resonate with the people in your audience at both an intellectual level and an emotional level, and quickly, you've lost them. Remember, we live in the age of distraction! People are besieged by e-mails, texts, and tweets, let alone their own thoughts and concerns. They could be doing five other things while you're talking.

A simple but powerful tool we use with our clients is called the *Audience Agenda System*. We challenge leaders to change their paradigm and engage in *180 Thinking*, meaning think like their audience. What does the person you will be speaking to want to know? Write down some of the key questions the members of your audience will have in mind when they are listening to you. Answer those questions first—especially what you would imagine to be the toughest question from the most skeptical audience member. Be sure you are answering their most important question: "So what?" Sounds simple, but we are always surprised by how many excellent leaders with great communication skills forget this important preparatory step. If you're not answering their so-what question up front, then start again. I can't emphasize this point too strongly.

Next, get to the point. Articulate your so-what message in crisp, succinct, jargon-free language that grabs their attention. Done correctly, your audience will sit up and want to know more. It's your Big Idea, and it's compelling. Think Steve Jobs, who mastered this technique and was so proficient at it that he made it look easy, just as the most talented pro athletes do when they perform an amazing feat.

Finally, give yourself the gift of feedback. The higher you rise in an organization, the less likely you are to get honest, direct feedback. So often, it's filtered or spun—hence the advent of a TV show like *Undercover Boss*. Start, then, by giving feedback to yourself. Use a mirror, a digital voice recorder, or a digital video device. Watch how you deliver your important message. What do you see? What do you hear? What's good? What requires additional thought? Note what you like about your delivery so you are confident when you are at the point of contact.

Note what you should work on. For instance, do you speak clearly? Are you conveying energy and enthusiasm? Does your message feel genuine? Are you believable? In other words, do you demonstrate conviction? Do you have to look at notes, or can you comfortably make eye contact with your audience as you are speaking? Do you have distracting mannerisms or vocal tics? Perhaps you say "umm" or "like" or "you know" too much. Be sure to identify all the elements of your delivery and your style that you want to improve.

Now find someone qualified to help you. The best athletes have the best coaches. We'll talk about the enormous importance of coaching and being coached in the next chapter. Few leaders in business today have the time, ability, and discipline to help themselves get to the highest levels of competence in the critical skill area that is communications. Just as you would seek out expert advice when pursuing a legal matter or resolving a medical concern, accept that you may need help. Then get that help.

BUILDING THE FIRE

The energy continuum is now complete. You have done the hard work to clarify your personal truths. You are courageously acting on them so your behaviors are now consistent with what you believe. This empowers you, and you now empower others. The resonating energy inside you has been mobilized. Armed with a better understanding of your organizational truths, you have cracked the code and identified the secret sauce that has or will set your company apart . . . or you have discovered the missing ingredient that it lacks. The atmosphere in your organization is rich with oxygen. A spark will ignite the energy and set off a chain reaction of exceptional forward progress. You know what the spark is—it's your simple, powerful, passionately conveyed message. Now you'll look around for the kindling. You'll need kindling to ignite the flames and make the fire spread and last.

Who are the disciples that will spread your powerful message quickly? Who are the ones whose own energy will be ignited by yours and who are a means to spreading the message quickly, efficiently, and effectively? If you faced a crisis such as the one I identified in this chapter, who would be three to five people in your organization you would rely on as the disciples who would spread your urgent message so it catches fire with the whole organization?

_____

_____

_____

_____

_____

WALK IN THE SHOES OF YOUR DISCIPLES

"Walk a mile in another man's shoes before you judge him." That's a proverb of apparently mysterious origin, and it resonates directly with the concept of the Audience Agenda System that I discussed in this chapter. I also reviewed expectancy theory and raised questions about whether most organizations truly understand the "desired outcomes" of the type of employees that flourish and create the results in high-energy cultures.

So now I'd like to ask you to reflect on the Pareto principle. Think about those top 5 to 20 percent of the employees in your organization—the peak performers, the self-reliant achievers. Walk a mile in their shoes. You need to really understand these people, as they are vital to your success as a leader and communicator. So engage in some 180 Thinking. Looking at things from their point of view, answer these tough questions:

- ▶ If I'm one of the best performers at this company, what *outcomes* result from my performance?

- ▶ Has anyone asked me lately what outcomes I value most?

- ▶ How often does management "preach to the converted" here as opposed to ignoring the best performers and focusing on the slackers?

- ▶ What actions has leadership taken in the last two months that focus on reaching for and celebrating team wins?

- ▶ How much do team wins result in shared rewards?

▶ If this company were to face a crisis, is my passion for our leaders so strong that I would walk through fire for them?

▶ What could our leaders do in the next two months to strengthen my sense that I am truly a valued disciple in this organization?

Don't be easy on yourself here. You can only save the "saved" if you're very honest about what you're doing right and what you could be doing better. And, if you sincerely aren't sure what the answers would be to some of these tough questions, then you really need to get some dialogues going—even if all is well on the surface at your company. Don't wait until an earthquake strikes before you have your foundation tested!

CHAPTER 11

Rise to Your Leadership Best

> *Circumstances do not rise to meet our expectations. Events happen as they do. People behave as they will. Embrace what you actually get.*
>
> —Epictetus, Greek sage and
> Stoic philosopher

For every great leader, there comes a crossroads that will test your ability to rise to the occasion.

Sir Ernest Shackleton's 22-month Antarctic journey from 1914 to 1916 is one of the ultimate testimonies to the importance of leadership under duress. It is an extreme example. Shackleton, a celebrated polar explorer during his time, aimed to be the first to cross the Antarctic continent, sea to sea, via the South Pole. In 1901, as a third officer on an earlier expedition to the South Pole, Shackleton was sent home for health reasons. This perceived failure and the fact that he had lost the race to reach the South Pole to the Norwegian explorer Roald Amundsen in 1912 fueled Shackleton's resolve to succeed on this unprecedented journey. The ill-fated trek became legendary because Shackleton led the stranded crew of 27 men through 22 months of near starvation, bitter cold, long months of complete darkness, and a series of demoralizing disasters. The physical and emotional stresses were almost incomprehensible, but the survivors' stories provide indisputable evidence that it was Shackleton's leadership that led to the crew's rescue. Despite the constant threat of frostbite and starvation and a harrowing attack by a 12-foot-long, 1,100-pound leopard seal, not a single man perished.

The examples of his timely leadership during the South Pole expedition are many. For instance, when their aptly named ship, the *Endurance*, became ice locked, Shackleton ordered his men to try every means possible to extricate it. Although the order proved futile, it proved to be a sagacious leadership decision. Because of the effort, none of the men could regret that they didn't try everything possible to free their ship before it was destroyed by the pressure from the ice. This liberated the crew from brooding on "what if." Shackleton was calm, confident, and courageous throughout the perilous months that followed. He led from the front, constantly checking on the health and well-being of his crew. Ultimately, he took five of his men on a high-risk journey in a lifeboat through frigid, tempestuous seas to reach a whaling station that was 800 miles away on a remote island. They reached land only after having to wait out a hurricane. If that weren't enough, they then trekked 26 more miles on foot across nearly impassable mountains and glaciers on the island to the whaling station. They managed this feat without climbing equipment. Once the group reached the whaling station, Shackleton immediately summoned a new crew and ship to return to rescue the rest of his men.

LEADING IN THE FACE OF CHALLENGES

Leadership is the act of leading. If you're a CEO, your working conditions are far superior to those endured by Shackleton. Still, your job is to lead your people to ever-increasing heights of success, ultimately measured by shareholder value, regardless of crises and obstacles. These will test your ability as a leader, and your legacy will be judged by the actions you choose to take to lead the people in and around your organization who must help.

When you are in the seat of leadership, challenges arise. Although they are rarely matters of life and death, they can be treacherous in their own regard. They could arise in the form of a significant change:

▶ The planned divestiture of an underperforming business unit

▶ An acquisition of or merger with another company

- Expansion into another part of the globe or into another market segment

- The launch of a new product or service

- The purchase and implementation of new technology or additional manufacturing capacity

- The reorganization of the corporate structure

These are just some of the events that will inevitably occur and challenge your ability to lead. These are planned events.

Then there are the unplanned events:

- A sudden product malfunction that puts consumers at grave risk

- A breach of confidential information

- An act of terrorism that directly affects your company and your people

- The unexpected financial demise of a large client

- A sudden shift in customer or market preferences

- The collapse of a country's monetary system that affects the global financial markets

- The bursting of an economic bubble and subsequent investor retreat

As Epictetus—a born slave who rose to become a philosopher— expressed so eloquently in the quote that opens this chapter—the key is your ability to *embrace what you actually get*. Difficulties are going to arise: But it's not the situation; it's how you handle it. How you lead when the significant challenges occur is critical because it defines who you really are. It demonstrates whether you are a leader like Shackleton or a sham. (A good example of the latter is British Petroleum chief executive Tony Hayward, whose leadership during the Deepwater Horizon oil spill is now iconic for poor decision making by a key leader during a crisis.)

Your response to critical challenges signifies your effectiveness, or lack thereof, as a leader. That is why the work you have done throughout the processes of the previous chapters is so critical. It has prepared you to be the leader that you are capable of being. So how you will lead during times of critical challenge or turmoil is more sharply focused. Your personal truths and the organization you've created and energized around you will respond. There no longer is a question. It is certain. Like the imperiled crew of the *Endurance*, your people will look to you for guidance. Like Sir Ernest, you will courageously and confidently navigate them through turbulent waters. The most significant factor that determines your organization's success or failure—your leadership—is now poised for greatness.

"The Guts of a Burglar"

Behaviors during challenging times are the truest indicators of what a leader really believes. Consider the legacy of Katharine Graham. At 46, out of a sense of duty, Katharine Graham thrust herself into the CEO seat of her family business, the *Washington Post*, upon the death of her husband, Philip. The year was 1963 and although Katharine had no experience running a company, she grew the business over the next twenty years into the fifth-largest publishing company in the nation. She made an enormous impact on the then male-dominated newspaper business, especially because she resided in the center of political power in the United States. To women, and to the United States public, Katharine became an important icon.

During her tenure, the challenges were many and difficult. Her shining moment came when she courageously chose to unveil the Watergate conspiracy that ultimately led to the resignation of President Richard Nixon. Graham presided over the *Post* when reporters Bob Woodward and Carl Bernstein brought the story to editor Benjamin Bradlee. Graham ultimately supported the investigative reporting of Woodward and Bernstein and chose to run the story. Years later in an interview with the *Washington Post*, Bradlee described Graham's leadership as "intensely loyal." "Once she made up her mind, she was incredibly supportive. She had the guts of a burglar, not scared of anybody."

Tough as she was, Graham had a remarkable ability to maintain friendships despite vastly different viewpoints on such contentious topics as politics. Her personal truths were, it seems, in part her mother's, who was a bohemian intellectual, art lover, and political activist, and was able to befriend people as diverse as Albert Einstein and Eleanor Roosevelt. Graham leveraged this skill and other instincts to learn to be an effective CEO. She led from her heart and felt compelled to succeed by an inner sense of duty to her family and society. Gandhi once said, "Without a journal [newspaper] you cannot unite a community." The same is true for a company or a nation, for that matter. During the most tumultuous of times, Katharine Graham was able to unite, revive, and grow a flailing conglomerate, as well as make enormous strides in gender equality at a time when there was little appetite for it.

Ironically, a large factor in her leadership brilliance was attributable to her self-doubt. In her memoirs, she speaks about her lack of confidence and often refers to her self-doubt as a reason for her self-determination. Ironically, these insecurities proved useful to her. They contributed to her ability to overcome difficulty, continue moving forward, and lead successfully. Katharine's skill at gaining the confidence of her most ardent detractors, including union officials, CIA leaders, and the most powerful male figures in journalism, emanated from her communication skills—namely, her "directness of expression." She spoke with a tough, unsentimental style that breathed life into her personal truths. These personal truths in action helped drive her success as a business leader in times of peace and in times of crisis. Her fundamental truths were summed up poignantly in her words of advice to other future leaders, "Love what you do and feel that it matters."

This is not only good advice from Ms. Graham; it represents a principle that universally applies. Whether you lead a large public company, a division or business unit, a department, a large private company, a small company, a not-for-profit company, a country, a church or temple, a city government, a football team, or a family, her words will always apply.

TO LEAD IS TO COACH, TO COACH IS TO LEAD

Perhaps one of the most important leadership competencies I ever learned was when my high school football coach taught me the "forearm shiver." While I never had the opportunity to use the forearm shiver as a leader—and it's not even legal on the football field anymore—the process of learning it provided me with a profound lesson.

When I was a sophomore on the varsity football team, Coach McCauley had high expectations for me. He had coached my brother Bob 11 years earlier, and Bob had set a rushing record that stood for over two decades in my hometown. And he did it as the quarterback! After testing me at quarterback, Coach McCauley quickly realized I had little of the talent my brother brought to sports. After several days of trying me at various skill positions, he finally put me on the offensive line. I was a tough guy, but I was slow and undersized and had never lifted weights. I always felt Coach saw something in me because he seemed *committed* to getting the most out of me.

He continued to try me at different roles, but for those first few weeks of training camp, I could see his frustration growing as he struggled to figure out what, if anything, I could contribute to the team. In some ways, the situation reminds me of what 1980 U.S. Olympic hockey coach Herb Brooks once said to former Boston University star Dave Silk in the early days of that legendary team: "I don't know if you *can't* skate, or if you *won't* skate, but I intend to find out!" Coach McCauley seemed determined to learn if I could have any utility on the football field.

One day, he asked me to stay after practice and meet him at "the sled." The seven-man sled was a dreaded contraption used to make linemen better at "firing off the ball," using proper form to drive the opponent off the line of scrimmage. Like most players, I hated the sled.

Coach McCauley and I were the only ones there this hot August morning. He said to me, "David, I thought you were more like your brother, but you're not."

I lowered my head. I knew it was true, but the words hurt.

"But," he went on to say, "you're tough, and I like that." I became encouraged. He continued, "I know you can lead this team if you learn a technique that will leverage your toughness and give you the advantage you need to excel." I was listening intently now. "I need you to lead this team someday, so I'm going to teach you the forearm shiver, David. You will become so good at this, it will be instinctual. When you master this technique, it will render your opponent helpless for just enough time for you to gain the advantage to either overpower him or get away from him to pursue the ball carrier."

He then proceeded to show me this devastating technique. Starting with my hands at waist level, I would make a quick, powerful step into the opponent while driving my dominant forearm up into the chin area with a fast and forceful motion. When executed correctly, the full power of my legs, hips, and shoulders would be behind the extended forearm.

He had me do this to the pads on the seven-man sled, slowly at first until I had perfected the motion. Then he ordered me to repeat the motion. "Do it 50 times quickly." Then he had me do it from a three-point stance while moving down the row of pads after each hit. We did this for what seemed to be a solid hour. I was exhausted, but I was thrilled. Something about the forearm shiver gave me a sense of power. And man, did it work! Coach had me practice this before and after each team session until it did become instinctive. I can still remember the sound it made on the pads of the sled. It was a loud "pop!" And when it was leveled on an unsuspecting opponent, the sound was even more satisfying. I used it consistently and, over time, expertly. No one could defend against it. By my senior year, I became all-league at offensive guard and all-county at middle linebacker. Coach McCauley had given me a tool to leverage my strength, alternatively minimizing my weaknesses.

Good leaders take a genuine interest in their disciples.
They patiently seek their strengths, and they coach them to
leverage their strengths to great success.

The coaching process is to teach first, encourage and guide, and then coach the individual to practice. Practice. Practice. Practice. A good coach challenges you to be the best you can be, and, sometimes, you resent her for it. Not forever, because when you look back on the experience, you invariably see it as one of the best learning experiences of your life—a time when you developed a skill that gave you confidence. Confidence propels you to higher levels of performance. A great performance raises everyone around you and increases the success of the team. Good coaches do this, and the best leaders are good coaches. (As a side note, Coach

McCauley did the same for my brother before me. He became Coach's protégé and had a fabulously successful and inspiring career as a player in high school and college and then as a coach himself. Armed with lessons learned from Coach McCauley, my brother Bob went on to become a coach in two Super Bowls in the NFL. Both he and I share an enormous affinity for Coach McCauley because of the personal interest he took in us. It has made an enormous difference in our lives. God rest his soul.)

A SIXTH SENSE FOR TIMING

Leaders who coach well develop leaders who perform well. Like Coach McCauley, great business leaders:

- Take a *genuine* interest in their people

- Commit themselves to helping potential leaders become better leaders

- Identify and focus on strengths versus weaknesses

- Provide meaningful guidance

- Speak from experience and wisdom

- Encourage, empower, enable, and energize

- Communicate with courage and tact—"courageous, considerate communication"

- Have a sixth sense for timing

That last bullet is the differentiator. Only the greatest leaders have this. The executive team around Neil Goldberg would often remark about Neil's ability to know exactly what to do and when to do it. And as we grew the company exponentially, he seemed to stay one step ahead of all of us somehow. We related this sixth sense to intelligence. Bill Gates put it this way: "[Smart] is an elusive concept. There's a certain sharpness, an ability to absorb new facts. To ask insightful questions. To relate to domains that may not seem connected at first. A certain creativity that allows people to be effective." This describes Neil's leadership prowess.

Doing all this right as a leader-coach will strengthen relations, deepen commitment, and foster self-motivation and personal development in those leaders around you.

Please remember the first rule of developing leaders: Development begins with people who are developable!

MORE ABOUT 180 THINKING

Why do you need to *embrace* leadership challenges? After all, no one goes around hoping for obstacles and crises. Still, challenges represent important opportunities for you as the leader as well as for the development of those emerging leaders around you. Have you ever been in a situation where your leader completely abandoned her stated truths in the midst of a crisis?

When I reflect on my own career as a leader, I realize that the single most important factor in my own leadership success has been focusing on my followers during times of difficulty. If there is any personal strength I can point to, it is a consistent behavior of *increasing* personal commitment to those I lead in times of difficulty. When the stakes are highest, I feel it is critically important that I watch their backs and guide them through the stormy seas with counsel, understanding, and sound, unambiguous decision making.

As noted in the previous chapter, we teach executives the powerful concept of "180 Thinking" at Bates Communications. We use this to help executives think from their audience's point of view. This is important when preparing a presentation or a speech, because unless you truly understand what is on the minds and in the hearts of the members of your audience first, you will have little chance of connecting with them. However, the same concept also applies when leading during challenging times. As a leader, you must act to understand what is on the minds and in the hearts of those disciples around you. They are the ones whose actions will determine success or failure. Focus on them first.

The time for building trust, identifying strengths, building competence through practice, and developing your team is all *before* the challenging time hits. During the challenge, you will reap the dividends of that shrewd investment. The extent to which you can leverage this investment will determine your effectiveness at preparing the team and building the foundation of a winning team. After the challenge, there is time to reflect, evaluate, learn, and plan. There is also time to make changes that emerge as necessary. The most significant challenges in my career as a leader are the most satisfying professional memories I have.

Adversity brings good people closer together. Relationships created during such difficult times and under such tough conditions often last a long time, even a lifetime. The events during these tough times become fodder in followers' memories of those days when they were, ironically, impacted favorably—when times that tried men's (and women's) souls made them who they are today . . . in a *good* way. At such times, other people's actions can change a person for the better. And they become part of the legends and folklore that perpetuate your high-energy culture.

A CALL TO ACTION

The opportunity is greatest during the inevitable twists and turns that occur during your time in the seat. These are the events that call for you to act. These are the times when people look to you for guidance. These are the moments when all the work you did or didn't do to prepare is brought to the forefront and on display for all to see. When significant challenges arise, do people look at you with faces of trust, respect, and hope? Are they waiting to hear your direction because they know that it will be sound and that doing their best to carry out whatever you decide is in their best interest and their beloved organization's? Or do they look at you because they have to? Do their expressions reveal exasperation and despair? Look into their eyes and determine which of these you see. Search your heart and soul. Be honest. What do you see?

The good news is you are now more capable than ever. You've done the hard work to declare your personal truths so that you are grounded by them. Ironically, in some ways you are more protected and in other ways more vulnerable than ever before. Remembering what is important to you will turn out to be invaluable. But like most measures of exper-tise, this is necessary but in no way sufficient. Leading at critical junctures requires skill and preparation. It requires the courage to act. And it requires effective communication.

It has been said that character is forged during crisis. Character is actually *revealed* during crisis. As a leader, your character has already been forged by the important people and experiences you have recalled over the course of your life. Crisis *is* your opportunity to reveal who you really are. Times of crisis are your moments to shine. Do not fear them. Embrace them.

More important, this is your purpose here on earth. Once you have accepted the responsibility and occupy the seat of leadership, you *must* act. You cannot waste moments of opportunity. More than just your reputation and your company's success are riding on it. Your people's potential to influence others and the world for current and future generations is riding on it. Your ability to help people change, grow, become better professionally and personally, and become the leaders of tomorrow is at stake as you navigate your company through these critical junctures.

I say this because I have witnessed it, and I say it because we heard it repeated like a mantra during the course of our five-year leadership development program. Enumerable examples of other leaders who had an impact on our leaders—either favorably or otherwise—came to light whenever our leaders shared memories of tribulations that they had experienced during their career. These memories are lifelong. They are what people recall because they are powerful. These are the events that shaped them. The leaders who rose to the call and made an impact on them are the people they write about when we ask, "Tell us about a time . . ."

A CAREER-CHANGING MISTAKE

At the request of the person who told me this story, I'm changing the identifying aspects of it in order to respect the privacy of the individuals involved. So this story is an *analogy* to something that really did happen rather than the literal truth. Suffice it to say, though, that what I'm about to tell you is a milder version of what really happened. This is the story of a really, really big mistake.

Executive Kevin Young was shaped by a major crisis that happened very early in his career . . . and by the way that his CEO responded to it. As a recent college graduate during a sluggish economy in the early 1980s, Kevin took the best job he could get. It was a low-level position for a major transportation company. Not the greatest job, but it was a start.

Kevin's primary job was to keep track of the massive amounts of raw materials that the company shipped across the country. As a convenient way to keep track of these incredibly large volumes, Kevin developed a little system. As it became cumbersome to continually write out the full weight of the coal, timber, and metals that had been procured, Kevin decided that he would record the number of pounds in hundreds. In other words, he would refer to "75" when alluding to 7,500 pounds of, say, aluminum.

Unfortunately, not everyone was aware of his "little system." As a result, the company ended up receiving a shipment of 90,000 pounds of steel—that's 45 tons—when all they wanted was 900 pounds! All hell broke loose. The warehouse was overloaded, and the company was now on the hook for a huge amount of money in accounts payable—not to mention the amount of overtime that would have to be paid for the warehouse workers to deal with the super-sized shipment. Across the company, people were frustrated and angry. Kevin felt awful about it. "What can I do to correct this?" he asked. "You've done enough!" his boss snapped. Very shortly thereafter, Kevin got the word that the CEO wanted to meet with him.

Kevin viewed his fate matter-of-factly. "The main thing that went through my mind as I awaited that meeting was this: *I wonder how it works when you get fired. Will they let me get my stuff myself, or will they just send it to me later?*"

Kevin sat down with his CEO, a highly accomplished gentleman who was a buddy of some of the biggest names in American industry. "I've been in this business for decades, and I've never seen someone at your level make a mistake of this magnitude," he said. "But you know what? I think that this is going to be a very valuable lesson for you."

Kevin nodded glumly. Then he said, "I'm sure you're right. My only question is whether I should clean out my desk myself or whether that will be taken care of for me."

The CEO cocked his head at Kevin quizzically before chuckling. "Kevin, you're not going to lose your job. I actually envy you. At this very early point in your career, you made a mistake that will be a powerful lesson for you for the rest of your professional life. So go back to work, and learn from that mistake. And I'm going to make a prediction right now: You are going to turn out to be a *pioneer* in the field of transportation management."

What a moment! Kevin took everything the wise CEO said to heart. He realized that he had treated the job as just a job rather than as a calling. He began devoting his evenings and weekends to *really* understanding the nuts and bolts of his field: inventory valuation methods, logistical principles such as responsiveness, sustainability, provisioning, you name it. And the prediction ultimately came true: Kevin is now an authority on logistical data and even gives keynote speeches on the topic.

But it all started with a major mistake . . . and a CEO who saw the opportunity in the crisis . . . and who responded in a way that led an employee at a crossroads to flourish in a high-energy culture.

YOU ARE IN THE DRIVER'S SEAT

How many executives would have responded as that CEO did? It would've been much easier to cast that entry-level employee aside like a crumb on the dinner table instead of seeing the diamond in the rough.

Perhaps nothing has surprised me more in my career than the realization that most leaders really don't understand the depth of responsibility they have accepted or how their actions, words, and behaviors impact the Kevins of the world. One of my primary purposes in life is to make sure that you do. Because it is important. And because I believe you have inside of you the means to change the world.

THORN, ROSE, AND BUD

We've been on quite a journey together through this book. If you've made a good-faith effort to not only read the book but try your hand at all or most of the exercises ending each chapter, I'm sure that the process has been an emotional roller coaster.

So as we move toward the end of this journey together, let's try to make sense of it all. Think of the process you've undertaken of taking a long look within as well as a close examination of the organization around you. You declared your personal truths and then tried to see if you could poke holes in them. You paid attention to the Alpha Dog and queried the key players. You cracked the code and identified your secret sauce—or the missing ingredient. Then you started to think about how to take this newfound knowledge and apply it to promoting and propagating a high-energy culture.

So reflect now on the journey and what you will take away from this book.

We want to take the time to smell the roses, but we also want to acknowledge their thorns:

1. Think about a low point of this journey. It could have been a difficult realization that struck you about how your personal truths compared with your organization's truths. Perhaps it was a sense of discouragement or disillusionment you felt as you found that your organization has a missing ingredient to its special sauce, or maybe it was a perception that you or your team lacks some essential component that you will need to be successful. Of all these possibilities, what proved to be your biggest *thorn*?

2. Now consider the high points of this journey. What was a eureka moment for you while reading this book—something that made your heart race and your mind reel because of some new revelation about leadership and communication? It might have been a legend or folklore that inspired you or an exercise that really made you pulse with resonating energy. In short, what was your *rose*?

3. Last, reflect on the challenges that await you in the months to come. We reviewed all sorts of processes and steps that you might undertake as a leader with your team. What are you most looking forward to trying out as you move forward? What are you most excited about as a tangible way to promote growth for you as a leader and for your team? This is your *bud*.

_____

_____

_____

_____

_____

WRITE YOUR OWN
LEADERSHIP "EULOGY"

On September 12, 2011, NPR broadcasted a story about "dignity therapy." It was about how psychiatrists have made various attempts to help people cope as they confront the reality of their impending death. What have they found? It's a theme similar to one that you've read about throughout this book: *Exploring our personal stories increases our ability to understand, grow, and change.* You could say that it's the ultimate opportunity for a paradigm shift: "When you face death, it's like facing a wall and it forces you to turn around and look at the life you've lived," says psychiatrist William Breitbart of the Sloan-Kettering Cancer Center.

With that in mind, I'd like you to imagine that you're facing that wall right now. From that perspective, turn around and look at the life you've lived. Consider this question: "What would you want said as your eulogy?"

Imagine that a time machine has transported you several decades into the future. The scene is a house of worship, packed with a congregation wearing somber colors. As you look around, you are stunned to realize that the pews are filled with your family members, friends, acquaintances, and colleagues—all considerably older but absolutely recognizable.

It hits you suddenly: This is your memorial service.

What you do as a leader during critical junctures determines how those who choose to follow you remember you as a leader. What will people who have followed you write about your leadership? What will be your professional legacy? Great leaders are the subject of this kind of reflection.

What do you want the eulogist to be able to say about you?

To help you along, I'll write the beginning of some sentences. Complete them in a way that is consistent with your personal truths.

1. "As we all reflect here today on our great loss, I want to say a few words about _____'s professional legacy. As an individual contributor, what made _____ different from the typical professional was _____

   _____

   _____."

2. "On a personal level, I know that many of _____'s colleagues and I have fond memories of our days together. As we worked together as a team, I always appreciated _____'s personal qualities of _____

   _____

   _____."

3. "As you know, _____ ultimately became a great leader. In order to energize their people, all leaders need to get off the fence and stand for something. Whether _____'s organization was enjoying great success or struggling through a challenge, I always knew deep in my bones that _____ stood for

   _____

   _____

   _____. There was never any doubt about that because that's what _____ was all about. That's why I'm proud to be here today to honor _____'s legacy as a leader."

Epilogue

*From describing the past, from the present which seized
my hand in its existed grasp, here I am, O future, now
mounting the crupper of your horse. What new pennants
wilt thou unfurl before me from towers of cities not yet
founded? What rivers of devastation set flowing over
castles and gardens I have loved? What unforeseeable
golden ages art thou preparing—ill-mastered,
indomitable harbinger of treasures dearly paid for, my
kingdom to be conquered, the future . . .*

—ITALO CALVINO, ITALIAN JOURNALIST
AND AUTHOR

My first memory of someone with powerful leadership energy was my grandfather. At age 16, Tomistacles Giammaria decided he was going to run away to America to pursue his dream. He left his small town in Italy, a village named Patrica in the mountain province of Frosinone about 50 miles south of Rome, and hopped a cargo ship. His plan was to find a distant relative who had emigrated from Italy earlier and settled in upstate New York. My grandfather was young, smart, courageous, and determined. Most important, he was a man with a dream and the passion to see it come to life. So upon arriving here, he immediately exercised his entrepreneurial spirit. His persistence paid off, and he became a success. Over time he was respected by most everyone in his small city. Later in his life, as a veteran of World War I, a city councilman, and a revered example to other intrepid pioneers around him who immigrated here to America with similar dreams, he became a trusted advisor and mentor. To his family, he was *the* leader and head coach.

My family's folklore is filled with stories of my grandfather's guts and savvy, but it was his *personal truths* and his *vision* that laid the foundation for all of us. These were personal truths he was willing to die for: that *freedom* is everyone's right and privilege here in America so he was free to build his business, to build a home for his family, and to do both wherever he chose; that the only path to success was through *service*—to his beloved family, to his new country, to God, and to others; and that *love* was unconditional for "blood" and those loyal to you. He had the courage to act on these truths.

The lasting presence of these truths through the generations is testament to the power of his character. A desire to succeed and a natural, inherent ability to lead were qualities upon which he built a career and a life as he grew up in America.

When I began to recognize how important writing this book was to me, and started organizing the concepts herein, I realized that my grandfather was at the beginning of it all. At a very early age, I recall wanting to be just like him. Now, as I look back and connect the dots of significant leadership events in my lifetime, my personal best leadership moments, I realize that my experience as a leader begins with what is inside me—the personal truths that my grandfather passed down to me:

Freedom. Service. Love.

These enduring beliefs formed early in my life, and they have shaped me over time like clay on the potter's wheel. They are *my* personal truths.

Whether we acknowledge it or not, all of us have within us a burning desire to do what we are here to do. We simply need to start by remembering what is important to us before we can get on with the work of doing what is important. Then we must muster the courage to act.

Do any of the following scenarios sound familiar to you?

1. You have reached a place in your career where you have position power and are earning an income that provides you and your family with an extraordinary quality of life. Perhaps you

are a CEO or have an impressive title and you're regarded by most everyone as a successful professional. By all traditional measures, you have "won." Yet privately you feel stuck. You wonder quietly why you don't feel as satisfied as you thought you would or should. Often, you have to force yourself to do the work because you have no idea what you can do to fix this feeling of being stuck.

2. Perhaps you are a leader in an organization that has been hit hard by the economic downturn. The cutbacks have been extensive, and another round is looming. The atmosphere is dominated by fear. People around you are more interested in finding ways to fly under the radar and protect themselves than to find ways to drive your business forward. You feel anxious and fearful yourself. The pressure and demands on you are building.

3. Or maybe you have become impatient as a leader. Neither the organization nor your people are moving forward at the speed you want. Things are okay . . . but could be so much better. You feel frustrated and de-energized. You are unclear on what to do to change this, to move your organization in the right direction.

4. You are between jobs. The opportunities for you are few, and you're at an age where companies may be quietly passing you over. You're wondering how you can find the right opportunity if no one gives you a chance.

5. Others whom you admire seem to have the courage to take control of their own destiny and act to courageously do something about it. You wonder what causes them to be willing to take the chance. Quietly, you wonder why you can't do the same.

The purpose of this book is to lift you out of these ruts. The premise, as you have seen, is simple:

You have the power within you.

The expectation is that by now you have begun to feel the power of this energy within. You are now responsible to do something with what you have learned. People are looking to you for guidance. You can no longer excuse yourself or shrink away from this responsibility. You must behave consistently with what you know is important. It is time to step up and don the mantle of the energized leader.

At the time of this writing, I frequently sit quietly in the nursing home where my parents now reside, while they live out their last moments. The slow, painful decline, like most challenges in life, has had one marginally redeeming quality for me. Nothing has been left unsaid. There are no regrets. I look at them both and realize their eulogies have already been written by the lives they have led. Their legacy is complete. They have both lived lives that they can be proud of, and everyone who knows them agrees. I wish the same for you.

I have learned this from them about leading such an enviable life . . .

It doesn't come by the grace of God alone. You have to go after it.

Index

About the Author

David Casullo has a passion for developing other leaders who have the courage and capability to *step up*, the desire to *learn and grow*, and the *commitment* to do whatever it takes to become their very best. David's experience helping leaders has consistently been recognized as remarkable. His own experience as a successful business leader and entrepreneur has given him credibility with executive leaders in the C-suite as well as with emerging leaders in key roles throughout many organizations. His style is quickly engaging and refreshingly genuine and promotes trustworthiness immediately.

Prior to joining Bates Communications, an international executive coaching and consulting firm in Wellesley, Massachusetts, David had been president of a successful multinational paper and packaging manufacturing business and senior vice president of human resources for a rapidly growing northeast megaretailer, Raymour & Flanigan. For 10 years, David's leadership and his leadership development initiatives helped Raymour & Flanigan become a billion-dollar retail giant, the largest furniture retailer in the Northeast and one of the fastest growing in the United States. He has also served as CEO and owner of two successful small businesses.

David is an energizing "grass-roots" leader who began his career in management in 1984 as the computer operations manager at a large Anheuser-Busch distributor. Always desiring to lead, he would welcome the opportunity to tackle the toughest business challenges head-on, taking him on a path of increasing leadership responsibility throughout his 27-year career.

David earned a bachelor's degree in math and computer science from Hamilton College in Clinton, New York, where he captained the varsity football team. He received an MBA from Rensselaer Polytechnic Institute in Troy, New York.

David resides in Boston and in Little Falls, New York, with his wife, Lori, of 26 years. They have been blessed with three wonderful children—Andrew, Jenna, and Sara.